OREGON THE WAY IT WAS

OREGON
THE WAY IT WAS

by

EDWIN D. CULP

The CAXTON PRINTERS, Ltd.
Caldwell, Idaho
1981

Library of Congress Cataloging in Publication Data

Culp, Edwin D.
  Oregon the way it was.

    1. Oregon — Description and travel — Views.
  2. Oregon — Social life and customs — Pictorial
  works. I. Title.
  F877.C84   979.5   81-1266
  ISBN 0-87004-285-8   AACR2

Lithographed and bound in the United States of America by
The Caxton Printers, Ltd., Caldwell, Idaho
137049

CONTENTS

ACKNOWLEDGEMENTS

To these people may I say thank you:

The excellent photographic work done by Charles Raymon Lindsay, a lifetime commercial photographer who copied and printed most of the photos in this book.

Fred Clark, owner of the Angelus Photographers of Portland.

Eloise Queen Ebert, Oregon State Librarian, and all of her helpful assistants.

Jack C. Murray, the Caxton representative, has been most helpful with his many worthwhile suggestions and improvements.

Florence Emma, my wife; Gail Ruth and Curtis Edward, our two children; and my brother, Richard Dean, all helped in some manner, including writing, checking, or running down needed information.

Salem: Lenta Caughell, Donald F. Dill, Stanley James Forrest, Marion Bretz Matujec, Doris Martin, Neva McCord, Howard Mader, Mary Minto, Margaret Pickett, Del Milne, Lloyd L. Craft, Connell Ward, Clark Moor Will, Luella M. Charlton.

Portland: Janet Binford, Merrill Femrite, George Kraus of the Southern Pacific, George J. Skorney of the Union Pacific, Edwin C. Haack, L. R. ("Bob") Knepper, John T. Labbe, Terry R. Parker, Margaret Watt Edwards, Thelma Bengs, H. Vor Halvorsen, R. A. Brouhard, Paul D. Hunt.

Woodburn: Eugene Stoller, Janet L. Sonnen, Alene Widmer, Joanna Wadsworth.

Corvallis: Gladys and Robert H. Hunt, Edgar A. Klippel.

Oregon City: Winifred and Dr. Wilmer Gardner.

Jacksonville: C. W. Burk.

Sumpter: Brooks Hawley.

Rockaway: Addison W. Lane.

INTRODUCTION

I was born in Oregon. My father and mother were born in Oregon. My wife and both our children were born in this state. We eat and breathe Oregon.

There is magic in the name. We OREGONIANS love it, honor it, and embrace it, but words seem inadequate to properly describe its wonders. It paints a picture of romance, discovery, mountains with snowy peaks, mighty untamed streams, vast stretches of plain and desert, great forests untrod by feet of man.

A hundred and fifty years ago Oregon was a land of primitive wilderness, thousands of miles from the populated areas along the East Coast of the United States. Its story has been partially told by gifted writers such as Washington Irving, Mark Twain, and Rudyard Kipling along with Oregon writers Frances Fuller Victor, Eva Emery Dye, and Stewart Holbrook. The Oregon name suggests to some a vision of trappers, miners, and cowboys along with friendly or warlike Indians. These things mark the Oregon country of yesterday.

Few states can boast a more glamorous or vivid past than Oregon's. Our earliest settlers came overland on horseback or on foot. Some came across the seas by sailing vessel, traveling around the southern tip of South America. Many came via covered wagon over the Oregon Trail. They were told about the vast stands of timber, mineral deposits of untold millions, soil rich enough to grow the best grain and seed, and sparkling rivers and streams loaded with fish. Even the words Oregon Trail stir and excite people. The covered wagon symbolizes Oregon because Oregon was always the dream at the end of the 2,000-mile trail — a weary trail fraught with hardship and peril.

The state was founded and developed by a strong, reliant stock of people — we call them OREGONIANS.

At the close of the great struggle between the states my grandparents, Southerners from Tennessee who had lost most of their worldly possessions, looked for a new life and felt the beckoning of the vast Oregon country.

There are many ways of approaching Oregon history. My interest has always been the pictorial one. I suppose people would say I'm visual-minded, as many of us are, by inhaling my history lesson with pictures. At an early age I showed a special fascination for illustrations offering a detailed account of crossing the plains, climbing the Rockies, and entering the Promised Land of the Willamette Valley in Oregon — the stories my grandparents had embedded in my thinking.

Collecting Oregon photographic postcards offered me the best pictorial description of our state available, at least within my price range. These early cards show how many of the little towns looked and how the people dressed fifty to one hundred years before I was born. They were the early OREGONIANS.

Edward H. Mitchell of San Francisco bought thousands of Oregon scenes from various local photographers such as Joseph Buchtel, Frank G. Abell, Peter Britt, and David Morton Averill and printed them on postcard stock for the general public. Edwin Cooke Patton and his brother, Harry David ("Hal") Patton, operated a postcard store in Salem. These men sent their own photographer to all sections of the state to photograph the unusual and fascinating scenery found only in the Pacific Northwest. Today the Patton cards are sought after by deltiologists (postcard collectors).

Some of the other cards I looked for were those taken by Walter Scott Bowman, famous photographer of the Pendleton Round-Up; Albert Lewis Thomas and Francis William Woodfield for their coastal shots; and Benjamin Arthur Gifford for his pictures of the Columbia River and boarding areas, including the world-famous Columbia River Highway.

I likewise found the stereoscope fascinating and secured all the Oregon views available. Carlton E. Watkins of San Francisco visited this state in 1867 and again in 1884 and has given us the photographic record of the Oregon Portage Railroad at Eagle Creek, where Bonneville Dam now stands. Some of the Watkins pictures were made in Oregon about the same time that Mathew Brady was taking pictures of the Civil War. Eastern photographers invaded the Oregon country, producing many photographs that found their way into the stereoscopic field. These included the Keystone View Company, B. W. Kilburn, Underwood & Underwood, and Darius Kinsey. Many of our own Oregon photographers made stereo views, including Crawford & Paxton of Harrisburg and later Albany, M. M. Hazeltine of Baker, C. M. Kester of Oregon City, C. C. Lewis of Monmouth, Frank Patterson of Hood River and later Ashland, and Woodard & Clark Company of Portland.

Of all the pictures I secured, nothing was more enjoyable to me than those from the Lewis & Clark World's Fair held in Portland in 1905. Part of my fascination was because my parents never grew tired of telling of the enjoyment they received from attending. The fair was not a world extravaganza, compared with other world's fairs, but it was a ball of fire in Oregon and especially in Portland. People who came to Oregon were surprised that Indians were not lurking around each corner. They were pleased with our temperate weather and found it a contrast to their Eastern heat. Most of all they liked, and soon learned to love, OREGONIANS. Postcards of this state were eagerly sought after, resulting in thousands of new people coming to make their home in this state.

I have been asked whether OREGONIANS are really different from other people. My immediate answer might be that they are, just as New Yorkers are different from people living in Texas. I pondered the question further and wished we might ask Harvey Whitefield Scott, the indomitable early editor of the *Oregonian*, or maybe Charles Arthur Sprague, former state governor and recent editor of the Salem *Statesman*. Both these men had keen vision and insight into such matters. I am continuing my interest in this subject. The *Oregon Almanac* in 1872 published a section headed "The Kind of People We Want to Come to Oregon," and it reads in part:

People accustomed to life in a new country, those who have the courage and pluck to go upon wild lands and among sparse settlements, to build up homes for themselves and families, will find in Oregon many inviting fields for their enterprise. Farmers of moderate means from the States of Mississippi valley or east of the Alleghany mountains, will find in Oregon good farms partially or wholly improved at low prices. Mechanics and laboring men usually have no difficulty in obtaining employment. The construction of railroads, just commenced at various points in the State, the great amount of building and other improvements going forward at the principal business centers, makes work for the laboring classes. And to such as have the wish to settle themselves permanently, the Government lands are open for preemption and homestead, only a few miles back from the present settlements.

The man of moderate capital will find in Oregon many openings for safe and permanent investments, in lands, in farming, or in manufacturing enterprises of various descriptions. Oregon needs population of all these classes. There is work and business here for many others, if they will but take hold of that which presents itself for honest hands to do at the time.

Female domestics are very much in demand, and can very readily obtain situations at from $20 to $30 per month for good, reliable and industrious house servants. For clerks, bookkeepers, and that class of persons generally, the field is very limited. Oregon can offer but little encouragement to adventurers of every class, men who live by their wits; for them there is nothing here to do. To be successful in Oregon it is absolutely essential that a man should pursue some regular legitimate vocation. Those who do this and do it well and faithfully, invariably succeed.

Harper's Weekly, printed in New York, on the last day of the year published a resumé of important happenings for the year 1859. We read about John Brown's raid into Virginia and problems in the Congress. Included is a summation of events about Napoleon and his problem with Italy, along with the continual uprisings in South America. It seems as though the news of the entire world is covered, but no mention can be found about Oregon becoming the thirty-third state to join the Union.

Many Eastern people who came West in the early days to become OREGONIANS found themselves part of another, infinitely distant world. The journey required four to six months of superhuman courage and backbreaking effort. It covered more than 2,000 miles of prairies, mountains, and desert. It aged people quickly and often killed off the weak. Portions of several diaries will illustrate this point.

From the diary of Mrs. J. T. Gowdy of Dayton, Oregon, written in 1852 and copied from the June 1940 *Oregonian:*

I thought The Dalles the most miserable place I ever saw. We had to give $25 a sack for flour and other things in proportion.

We had to go from The Dalles to the Cascades in flatboats, the cattle being driven over a pack trail to the mouth of the Sandy River.

By 1852 flatboats were operating for hire between The Dalles and The Cascades. Steamboats were operating below The Cascades or lower river. Earlier parties of immigrants had to travel down the Columbia on rafts which they built of logs cut at considerable distance from the river.

The day before we left we moved down to the brink of the river and slept in our tent. With the wagons torn up we had to all, sick and well, sleep in one tent. The next morning we were up early; made a breakfast of cold bread and meat with a cup of hot coffee. We climbed on board with the sick on beds spread out on top of everything. We couldn't cook on the boat, so we had to take cold food along.

They took the wagons to pieces, tied the running gear of each together and took off the covers. They put the running gear in the bottom of the boats, set the wagon boxes on the top, then packed people "like sardines in a box" on top of all that.

When we got out in mid stream they found we were too heavily laden and were in danger of sinking. Some of the women were panic-stricken and screamed. They landed us five miles below The Dalles on a narrow sandy beach with a high wood-bluff back of us.

When we started down the river again we were heavily loaded and the wind blew up the river so strongly we ran across and landed on the Washington Side.

The strong prevailing upstream wind was one of the difficulties regularly encountered by pioneers traveling down the Columbia River.

I think we only stayed there one night; we slept on the boat, just tumbled down anywhere we could. We cooked on the river bank.

I thought there could not be a worse place than The Dalles but when we got to the Upper Cascades I knew there could be. People by the hundreds were crowded on a narrow strip of land at the brink of the river with a high rocky cliff at the back.

We stayed there for some time waiting for the boys and oxen. When they came they put the wagons together and piled things in and went around the portage to the Lower Cascades a distance of five miles. We children walked all the way.

When we came around the falls to the Lower Cascades they had to take the wagons apart again, load them and ourselves on another flatboat. We stayed there a week or more at the Cascades waiting for a boat but it wasn't quite as bad as the Upper Cascades.

After a week, perhaps, we loaded onto another flatboat which landed us at the mouth of the Sandy River. The boys and girls and cattle were there. They put the wagons together, piled everything in, hitched up the oxen and we pursued our weary journey on to Portland and thence on to Salem.

Dr. William R. Allen writes home to his brother in the East telling some of his experiences, cost of living, and way of life in Oregon *(Spectator,* February 19, 1916):

Oregon City
May 4, 1851

I left home on May 15th last, traveled nearly twenty-five hundred miles across the plains and sandy desert, and encountered storm, wild tribes of Indians and the worst of all, the fell destroyer, Asiatic cholera with which disease about two or three thousand poor emigrants perished.

In October about 15th we got into the Cascade Mountains about one hundred miles from Oregon City, when the snow fell about two feet deep, covering all the grass that grows in those lofty mountains. In consequence, our cattle nearly all perished. Here was a tug of war — about 60 or 70 wagons, six or seven hundred head of cattle lost. I lost two wagons from $150 to $200. These, if I had got them through, would have made me feel comfortable. It was snowing such flakes as you never saw fall, nine-tenths of the persons frightened nearly to death. I as their captain and general advisor, walking around as a good general should, stimulating them to action.

I immediately started runners into Oregon City in the valley of the Willamette River to inform the citizens that there were a great many disheartened emigrants that were about to perish in the mountains. In the meantime, we made ourselves as comfortable as the nature of the case would allow. The third day the growing scarcity of our provisions caused considerable alarm. We had one bull left, which had stood the storm, and we were keeping him in reserve.

I talked to my men like this: "Gentlemen, God only knows when we will get out of these mountains, we may all perish. The snow falls here to the depth of two or three hundred feet. All egress and ingress may be cut off. In that event these cattle may save our lives. If you are willing to let perhaps the last chance slip of getting something to keep ourselves and children from perishing, you can do so. I am not. My advice is: Boys to your guns. Surround that bunch of cattle; shoot down some of them; guard the balance until we see further."

In one hour from that time my family had plenty of fat beef. In about ten days the news had been received at the city, a subscription of some $5000 was raised in the course of three hours, and men, horses and provisions and some brandy were in our camps. We all arrived in Oregon City on October 28, all well, without clothes. I with $150 in pocket and glad to escape with the loss of everything we had.

Well, there we were. House rent for a single room was from $25 to $75 per month; provisions were enormously high: Flour $75 per barrel; beef 16 to 18 cents per pound; potatoes $2.50 to $3.00 per bushel; bacon 30 to 50 cents per pound; sugar 25 to 30 cents; coffee 37½ cents; butter fresh $1; eggs 75¢ to $1 per dozen. You may suppose how small my $150 felt in my pocket. Everything to buy — furniture and the commonest kind, very dear; ordinary bedstead $16; a small breakfast table $40; in short, everything high.

I got a good house, put up some stickfast, made, or rather my wife made the table; bought a half dozen chairs and the cheapest I could find for $22.50; bought five bushels of potatoes for $15.00; 100 pounds of flour for $7.50; sugar, coffee and some cooking utensils and the cheapest I could live was $100 per month. Well something had to be done. The $150 was nearly gone.

In a week or two I got a call to see a sick woman — went to see her twice, charged them $25. It was several days before she was able to work. I was told "Doctor you must charge more than that or you can't live in this country." Rose [their hired hand] went washing for persons at $3 per day and some days she washed at home by the dozen pieces at $3 per dozen, making from $6 to $12 per day. My wife got some sewing at which she made from $1.50 to $2.50 per day.

Well, pretty soon Christmas came — a ball came on — no music to be had. Some persons who had heard me playing on the plains informed the proprietor that Dr. Allen was the best violin player in the territory, so they came to employ me to play. I told them I would play for $50. A gentleman from New York assisted me, playing second, for which he got $50. Toward close of the ball, I concluded to shake my leg once, after which the younger ones insisted that I should give them a few lessons in dancing. Thirteen lessons in six weeks for which I charged $200. The last night I gave a small cotillion party making in the operation, school and party $250. There was a ball for which I played alone $50; and two balls at a little town called Milwaukie, at which I made $50 each; two small parties at which I charged $25 each. Cured a man and wife of minor complaint for which I charged $50 — a poor man — such cases are worth $50 each. So you see, I am not idle in the vineyard.

The plain fact is, the practice of medicine is worth little. In Oregon there is very little sickness. It is said that they have to go east of the mountains to die at all. I have been in Oregon six months and I have seen less sickness than I ever saw in the same time in any other place in my life. Well, putting this and that together, my expenses, as I must live, are $100 per month. I have now in the house $500 in gold, some $50 gold pieces, some bullion, some chunks of gold. The interest on what I have loaned out is $1.25 a day. I have four oxen which I bought to sell. They are worth $75 each at this time. There have been new mines discovered in Oregon near the California line and nearly everyone is gone. The discovery was made on the Klamath River 300 or 400 miles from here. I am not sure but I shall go in three or four weeks. Otherwise I shall take an interest in a steamboat that is being built here. I told them I would put in $1500 provided they would give me $150 per month as clerk. They say they will do it. I cannot say yet which I will do.

The climate is the most delightful one in the world — the weather for some time after my arrival in this country was fine. The rains commenced sometime in November, then for about four months it rained every four days out of five, that is to say it rained some days very little and other days all day. It never rains hard in this country. When it begins to rain, the grass begins to grow and grows all winter. Stock requires no feed in this country, summer or winter. Beef is brought in from the plains at all seasons — the fattest you ever saw. Hogs the same. Some of the settlers have herds of Spanish cattle 2000 and 3000; some have Indian brood mares. Everything of the vegetable line that we have at home grows well here, except corn. They raise a little for roasting ears. I however have seen but one ear since I have been in Oregon. The finest wheat you ever saw. I left Missouri and care but little if I never see it anymore. They sow wheat at all seasons of the year; harvest all the summer and fall. They get two or three crops from one sowing. As soon as they get the wheat off they brush it and let it go for another crop. The second crop is good wheat. Onions are a great crop in this country. The ground is prepared and seed sown broadcast. They produce abundantly. Onions as large as a coffee cup worth in the fall $6 to $8 a bushel.

There are some large farms in the country, say from 300 to 500 acres, but I believe a majority will come under 20 acres — that is in cultivation. A man with 15 acres sowed in onions, potatoes and oats will make more clear money in one year than any farmer in Marion City. Oats are worth more in this country that wheat. Wheat is worth $1.75 to $2 per bushel; oats $2.50 to $3 per bushel. Turnips grow to the enormous size of 36 pounds; the largest I saw last winter weighed 15 to 20 pounds and one that weighed 36 and some ounces.

The weather is now getting warm; the nights in the warmest weather in summer are cool enough to sleep under a blanket comfortably.

Notwithstanding the abundance of Spanish cattle in the country, a good American cow is worth from $75 to $100, a good American mare from $200 to $300, a good yoke of cattle from $175 to $200.

The new gold mines are paying now an average of from $8 to $10 a day, so say authentic reports.

Affectionately your brother,
William R. Allen

F. M. Wilkins describes his trip on the Willamette River from Harrisburg to Portland in 1867 (*Oregonian,* January 1934):

On New Year's eve 1867 I landed in Portland by river steamer from Harrisburg. It was just about dark and the coal oil lamps were being lighted in buildings along the waterfront and in the old St. Charles Hotel. Our boat, The Enterprise, had been three whole days coming from Harrisburg. River steamers burned wood in those days and had been delayed on the first part of our run because men under contract to cut our wood and pile it along the bank had somehow failed to do so.

Just above the town of Peoria we had to tie up while deck-hands cut and brought fuel on board so that our first night was spent at Peoria not more than 12 or 15 miles below our starting point.

Our second night and tie-up was about at Champoeg and neither night was good for sleeping because we had brought along one cow and two horses. The horses stomped and champed all night and the cow bawled continuously for the calf she had left at Harrisburg.

At the Oregon City falls our boat went into a kind of canal made of piling and stone and plank to drop her grain and other freight into a chute that carried them to another boat below the falls. We six passengers walked down a flight of steps to the waiting boat.*

It was in the evening of the last day in December 1867 that we tied up at Portland. I was only 19 at the time and there were no cabs nor baggage toters but I made my way to the St. Charles Hotel.

I went to bed at the hotel. At Midnight I was startled by a terrifying sound of whistles and of bells tolling. I hurried into my clothes and ran down

---

*The Willamette canal and locks around the falls at Oregon City did not open until January 1, 1873.

the one flight of stairs, sure that the whole city was burning. The man behind the desk told me that Portland was ringing out the old year and ringing in the new, to go back to bed. I did but not to sleep.

The St. Charles charged me 25¢ for my bed and 25¢ for each meal. This seemed extravagant to me so I found a place to board for $5 a week.

WHEN AND HOW TO GO TO OREGON
(Oregon Railway & Navigation Company publication of 1880)

Spring is by all means the best season; the next, summer; the next, autumn; and midwinter the worst, for the journey to Oregon. In the spring the chances of finding employment are better than at any other time of the year; and the purchasers or renters of land can immediately proceed with its cultivation.

Emigrants from Eastern Canada and the Atlantic States have the choice between two routes to Oregon. One is by the steamers of the Pacific Mail Steamship Company, from New York to Colon (Aspinwall), thence by rail to Panama, thence by steamer to San Francisco, and thence by steamer of the Oregon Steamship Company to Portland, Or. The other is by rail all the way to San Francisco, over the Pacific Railways, and thence to Portland, Or., as on the former route. The Panama route is cheaper, especially for families, cooked food being provided by the steamship companies; but the journey from New York to San Francisco over it takes about a week longer than by rail. The overland route is preferable for emigrants from the Middle, Western, and South-western States.

Portland is reached from San Francisco by steamers of the Oregon Steamship Company, which leave the first-named port every five days. Steamers are large, new, and fitted with all the conveniences and luxuries of modern first-class steamships. The trip is made in from forty-seven to fifty-two hours, and affords the traveller full opportunity to enjoy the great scenic beauty of the Lower Columbia River. Leaving the Oregon branch of the Central Pacific Railroad at Redding, Cal., stages can be taken for Roseburg, the present southern terminus of the Oregon and California Railroad. Passengers by this route leave Roseburg in the morning, and reach Portland the same evening, passing through the Umpqua and Willamette Valleys. Two hundred and eighty-five miles of staging are required by this route.

Once at Portland, the traveller is within easy reach of all parts of Oregon and Washington Territory. Steamers of Oregon Steam Navigation Company leave Portland daily for all Columbia-river points, connecting at Kalama with the Northern Pacific Railroad, and at Wallula with the Walla Walla and Columbia-river Railroad. Except during low water, these steamers run up the Snake River to Lewiston. Connecting stage-lines assure easy transportation from various points on the Upper Columbia to *all* points in Eastern Oregon.

Immigrants, on arrival at Portland, will do well to call at office of Oregon

Railway and Navigation Company, where maps showing on enlarged scale all government and railroad lands are open to examination, and full information touching localities will be freely furnished.

But one class of tickets (first-class) are sold over river lines: a liberal allowance is made for baggage and household effects.

Passage-tickets at the present time, Feb. 1, by steamer from New York to San Francisco, are, cabin, seventy-five dollars; steerage, thirty-five dollars. Subject to changes in competition with overland routes.

Those who go over land will, in every case, save money by purchasing through-tickets. Railroad fares of the different classes to Portland, Or., from the different Atlantic seaboard and interior cities, are constantly changing. Emigrant through-tickets at the present time are, *via* San Francisco and Oregon Steamship Company:

New York, N.Y. $75.00
Chicago, Ill. $65.00

The stage route from Northern California to Oregon can be recommended to persons of means. Fare from Sacramento to Redding, the northernmost railroad station in California (a hundred and eighty miles), eight dollars; from Redding to Portland, four hundred and eighty miles (two hundred and eighty by stage, and two hundred *via* Oregon and California Railroad), forty dollars.

NEWS ITEMS
The Next State
Reprinted from the Albany, N.Y. *Knickerbocker,* October 21, 1851

The next State that will knock for admission will be Oregon. Since April last, a stream of immigration has been pouring in upon her of such volume as must soon make her fit to take a seat in the Senate. From January up to last dates, the arrivals from the East have amounted to over ten thousand. This, added to the thirteen thousand she had last fall when the census was taken, makes her present population — counting the babies which have arrived since the census was taken — about twenty-five thousand. The people who go to Oregon are hard-fisted farmers, men who prefer the certainty of yellow corn to the allurements of gold or the temptations of California. The difference between the population of Oregon and that of California is just the difference between a cart horse and a racer. One is all utility, and the other all excitement. California will always have the most roulette tables, but Oregon will have the most mills. With the single exception of gold dust, Oregon has more natural advantages than any other country in the world. With a climate as fine as that of Virginia or Maryland, it can brag of a soil whose richness will challenge comparison with that of the inexhaustible prairie. In the way of timber, no country on earth can approach it, consequently it is destined to become the great lumber region of the Pacific. The distance, which formerly frightened people from seeking a home in Oregon, steam has reduced to a pleasure trip. By means of Vanderbilt's new line of steamers, people can go from new York to Oregon in less than five weeks. Three years ago it took from six to nine months. In addition to agricultural and lumber riches, Oregon is singularly blessed with mineral wealth. On the Columbia, iron ore exists in almost endless quantities, and the same may be said of copper, platina, lead, plumbago, sulphur and salt. To develop the productiveness of these treasures, all that is required is time and population. The former is coming along now, and the latter will be in a year or two. To men of patience and perserverance, there is no portion of our glorious country which holds out more prosperous inducements than Oregon. The Vice President will please see that two more chairs are immediately added to the Senate Chamber. If they are not needed this season, they will be by the year 1854.

In 1912 Gov. Oswald West rode horseback, strictly western cowboy style, from the Willamette Valley in western Oregon to the Idaho border, where he was met by the governor of that state. He roughed it like any westerner would. As a true OREGONIAN he wanted to see the interior of his great state. Rail service had not yet reached the interior, and the average roads were not much more than trails. He described his trip to an *Oregonian* reporter:

There were times, when passing through the more isolated country that I went for as long as a day and a half without seeing a person or passing a settlement or farm. I averaged between 30 and 40 miles a day but always took my time. At no stage of the trip was I lonesome in the least; and while I often found the weather a little uncomfortable, it was neither too hot nor too cold to delay my progress. When I did reach the more thickly settled parts of the country I was given a royal welcome and the people could not do too much to make my stay pleasant. I have no regrets. I believe that it was a sort of vacation. It furnished information that I wanted as well as giving me an insight into the resources of the great state of Oregon.

Do we understand OREGONIANS any better now? Are they really different from other people? The problem was getting too big for us, so we reached out to some well-recognized living OREGONIANS for their contribution on this heavy question. Thomas Lawson McCall, our former Governor, gives us his thoughts on this subject:

Your average OREGONIAN likes his or her state tremendously and proves it by helping to keep it clean and green. He sees that land and some other resources are finite and so favors wise growth to growth for growth's sake. He is a conservative progressive; that is, he is not opposed to innovation, but he wants to have an idea of where it leads before he approves of starting out. He's a good neighbor and kind to man and beast alike. He loves beauty, in nature and in manmade things. He is independent politically, and his vote is unpredictable, except that he votes for the candidate a lot more often than mere party label. To sum it all up . . . don't take an OREGONIAN for granted.

Leo George Spitzbart managed Oregon's great State Fair for more than twenty years; he surely must know all about OREGONIANS. He wrote:

What is an OREGONIAN? How do you become an OREGONIAN? Not that it matters to anyone else but I am an OREGONIAN of long standing. It happened this way. In 1900 my Father grew tired of the way the weather bureau in Iowa was running things; somehow he heard that Adam and Eve had lost Paradise — that was bad. Sometime later Lewis and Clark came west and found it — that was good. Being four years old, and having trust in my Father's judgment, I followed him to the center of the good world, to the Willamette Valley. Lest this savor of Chamber of Commerce propaganda, in the past 76 years I have found it to be all true. Sure we have an occasional shower, but mostly it's a damp dry drizzle. Some people dry their clothes in it. How else could we have the lush greenery, the beautiful streams and the most salubrious climate in the world? If this sounds provincial, let me quote from a widely travelled highly intelligent TV great, David M. Brinkley, who after several trips to Oregon said: "The beauty of it — the openness of it — the cleanness of it — the people are nice — what else is there?"

The Portland *Oregonian* has been the leading newspaper in this state for many years, so surely Editor John Richard Nokes can help us. Here's his report:

An OREGONIAN is a peculiar critter. He is wet on the west side and dry on the east; he is the sand of the beach and snow of the mountains. He is verdant valleys and parched deserts. He came by covered wagon and train and automobile and jet plane. He came from the midwest and the south; from the eastern seaboard and Latin America; from Hollywood and from China. He came from farms and ghettoes; from tribes before the white man and from jungles of Africa. He came from the countries of Europe. He is an intellectual and a farmer; a boss and a worker. He is religious and irreligious. He is a conservative and a liberal. Most of all he's a cantankerous independent. A motto from America's Revolutionary War suits him well: "Don't Tread on Me!"

Are you an OREGONIAN or do you just wish you were?

SALEM

Salem, 12:30 P.M. Wednesday, October 8, 1873: Ceremony of laying the cornerstone for the state capitol by Masonic Grand Lodge of Oregon. The stone was placed in the northwest corner of the building by Most Worshipful Grand Master Thomas McFadden Patton. So much interest was shown by Oregon people that the Oregon & California Railroad operated a special train from Portland to Salem. This was the second capitol at this location. Today the third capitol occupies approximately the same location as the other two buildings.

Edward Sexton Lamport and wife in their 1910 Pullman automobile. In the backseat are their two sons, Frederick and Merrill. Car cost about $3,000 and went out of production in 1917. Capitol building in background.

Big parade and Republican rally in 1902 — GOP working to elect James Withycombe governor. Note streamer extending across the road from the YMCA building for George Earle Chamberlain, a Democrat. The Democrats won the election, but Withycombe was elected governor at a later date.

Salem July 1894: An early post office scene when it was located at Commercial and Ferry streets. Note *Capitol Journal*, left, one of Salem's daily newspapers. Postal employees are (left to right) Murray Gilbert, Mollie Creighton, Zaidu Palmer, Scott Bozorth, Ben Taylor, Fred Lockley, Charles Cosper, George Hatch, and John Wright, grocer, on end. (Fred Lockley's profession was journalism. He has written many worthwhile books about the state. He probably is best known for "Observations of the *Journal* man," a column that appeared in the Portland paper for many years. Material for this column was made from interviews with Oregon people.)

State Street looking east in 1918. (Left to right) Masonic Temple; courthouse, which was dismantled in 1952; post office, moved in 1938 to become Gatke Hall for Willamette University; and dome of state capitol building destroyed by fire in 1935.

Trade Street in 1891. The railroad spur track, with small, diamond-stack locomotive shown here, connected the Southern Pacific main line with industries located along the Willamette River waterfront. In the background is the capitol building, which was without a dome until 1892. Electric power was generated in the plant near the center of the picture. Piles of cordwood were for purchase and delivery to the people of Salem for heating their homes.

August C. Schaffer and helper in their shop at 404 South Commercial Street in Salem in 1915. City directory for that date called their operation a "horseshoers shop" and not a blacksmith shop. Today's location would be across the street from Boise Cascade Corporation.

Salem 1910: John Minto, photographed with his imported purebred Merino sheep, which he kept on privately owned Minto Island, a peninsula between the slough and the main channel of the Willamette River. (John Minto, 1822-1915, was many things in his lifetime, including coal miner, mountain explorer, road builder, legislator, historian, and poet. He was truly one of Oregon's great.

27

Salem 1910: Ben Taylor, a Salem postman, and Dr. H. H. Scovell, a local mechano-therapeutist, built this airplane in 1910. On June 14 it was taken to the fairgrounds for testing and, with Dr. Scovell at the controls, barely cleared the ground. After three unsuccessful attempts at flight and three crashes it was retired to become a State Fair exhibit. Folks from the boondocks paid two bits for a look at this flying machine that wouldn't fly and to hear its thirty horsepower motor roar.

"Free Cigar Boxes" from Frank William Waters Cigar Store in Salem in 1908.
Fred Palmer and Bice Madison in background.

Benjamin Isaac Maxwell (1898-1967) on assignment for one of his many historical writings. He was often referred to as "The Sage of Polk County." His photographic genius was unexcelled; his writings will be a legacy for future historians. Years before his passing Ben wrote of himself "Accomplishments small; hobbies none; joys few." Everybody knew it wasn't so.

The annual Cherry Fair in Salem was an important event. Scene taken in 1914, with the home of Gov. Zenas Ferry Moody in the background. Those shown on float are (left to right) "King Bing," believed to be Chandler Percy Brown; two small boys pulling, Deryl Franklin Myers and John Douglas Minto; "Queen Ann," Mildred Roberts Palmer; two small girls, Mabel Louise ("Billie") Cupper and Maxine May Myers Claggett; four girls standing, Florence Cartright Sewall, Maxine Buren, Alice Rosalie Buren, and Catherine Hartley.

Patton Bros. Book Store was located next door to Ladd & Bush Bank Building in Salem. (Left to right) Maude Robinson, August Neugebauer, Harry David ("Hal D.") Patton, Edwin Cooke Patton, Virgil A. Anderson, Gertie M. Capps.

A big chess game held in the back room of Steiner's Drug Store in Salem in 1899. Those playing and watching are Lee Steiner, Matt Brown, Edward Hirsch, Armint Steiner, J. J. Wilson, H. John Bigger, Albert Steiner.

The Edwin Cooke Patton family in their new 1915 Studebaker touring car, with a side view of the Cooke-Patton home in background. House was removed, and the Oregon State Library is now on same location. Backseat (left to right): Mrs. Leah Orsella Guiss Patton and Miss Andrea Ipson; driving, Mrs. Luella May Patton Charlton.

Salem (opposite page): Edwin Nathaniel Cooke home built in the 1870s at a cost of $50,000. The lot was purchased for $1,500 from Octavious Manthano Pringle. Architect for the home was A. Burton, father-in-law of Henry Lewis Pittock, owner of the Portland *Oregonian*. The home was by far the finest and most prominent mansion in Salem. It was dismantled in 1938 to make way for the Oregon State Library. (Above) The parlor of the Cooke mansion, showing Mrs. Eliza van der Cooke, wife of E. N. Cooke. (Edwin Nathaniel Cooke was Oregon's second secretary of state. Octavius Manthano Pringle was the grandson of Tabitha Moffett Brown, one of the founders of Pacific University at Forest Grove.)

"Clang, clang, clang, goes the bell" at each revolution of the wheel, as Willard Dorance Pettingell makes the rounds of the city of Salem sharpening scissors and knives about 1900. His son, George Pettingell, operated an electrical shop in Salem for many years.

Joseph B. Underwood was reported to have owned and operated the first automotive taxicab in Marion County, a 1912 Model T Ford town sedan. Note wood on curb to be used for winter heat.

Ray Stormont and John Gordon, bicyclists, stop off in Salem in 1912 en route to New York City. Note Oregon state capitol in background.

President Theodore Roosevelt visited Salem during May 1903 and spoke from the porch of the statehouse. Following his speech he was accompanied by Oregon Gov. George Earle Chamberlain, in soft hat and to the president's right. State capitol in background.

Winter wood was delivered in four-foot lengths. The wood-saw man then cut it into 12-inch lengths. Henry Lyman Briggs, a local inventor in Salem and head of the H. L. Briggs Manufacturing Company, worked out an arrangement for cutting wood by using his 1911 Model T Ford.

A 1912 standard touring automobile driven from the Capital City Garage of Salem by John Charles Nicholsen. The garage, located at 173 South Liberty Street, is managed by A. V. Clay and B. G. Boedigheimer.

City of Salem, stern-wheeler, ready to leave from Trade Street dock on the Willamette River, Salem 1885, with the Salem Home Amusement Club Band shown on the upper deck. Capt. George Raabe is in the pilot house.

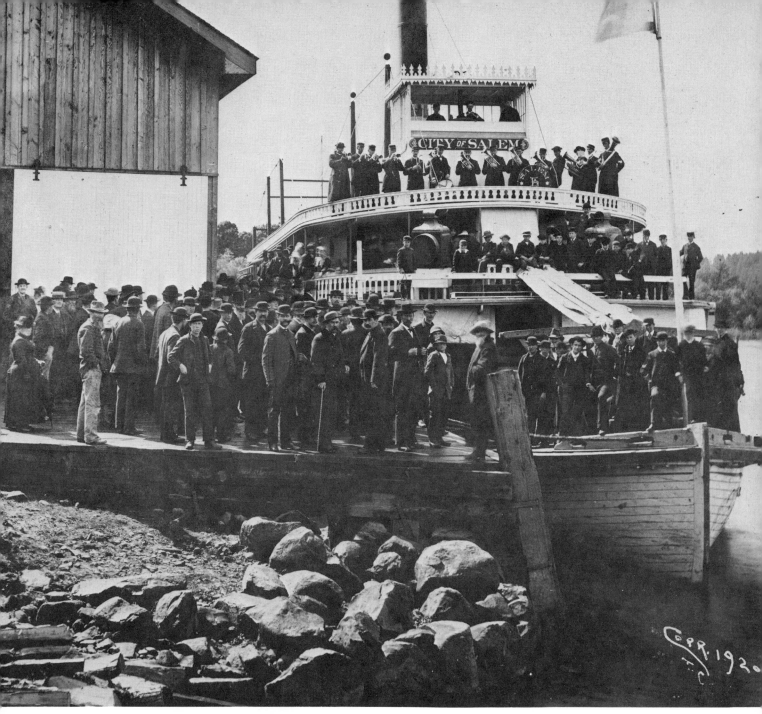

William Howard Taft, president of the United States, shown standing, visited Salem in 1911. Seated are Mayor Louis Lachmund and Gov. Oswald West. Grace W. Wheelock, public school music teacher, directs Salem school children singing "America." House in background is Breymen-Boise home on Court Street, now dismantled with service station on same corner. Note Secret Service men surrounding the 1910 Pierce Great Arrow automobile.

PORTLAND

The hottest days were always delightful under the shade of
the stately old oak trees in the park.

Portland 1905: Washington Park and Zoo, situated on the edge of the western hills and near Council Crest. In 1871 the city purchased a forty-acre tract for a city park, and eventually this was increased to 100 acres. This early scene in the park shows people feeding the bears.

The park borders the Willamette River. Picnic grounds are still beautiful at The Oaks, and amusements for children and grown-ups still attract, but the bathhouse and swimmers are gone, as pollution of the river makes swimming only a memory. These scenes taken in 1922 show Mrs. Charles Chester Renfro and two children enjoying the swim.

The Oaks, Portland's oldest amusement park, has been in constant use since 1905. Hundreds of people would board the interurban cars for a Sunday outing at The Oaks. Riding in the open trailer cars was the start of a very pleasant day (below).

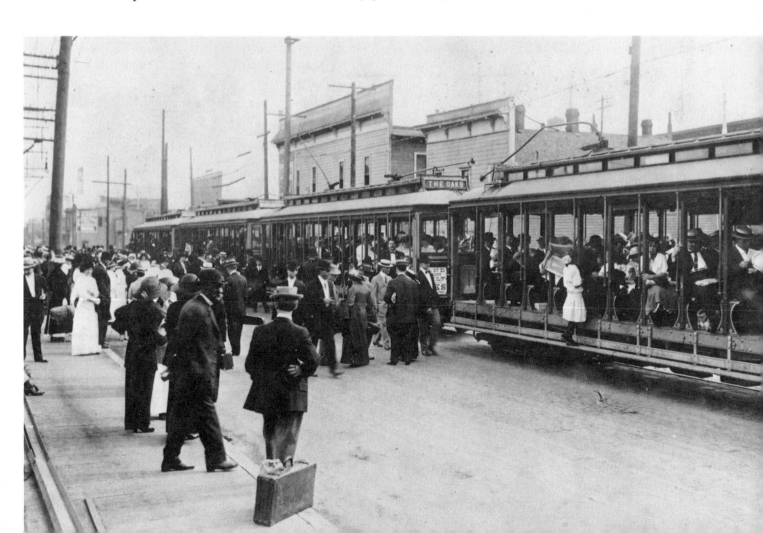

Portland Crematorium about 1900: Horse-drawn hearse shown in front of the Portland Crematorium.

Portland 1904: Portland Public Baths. This large swimming tank was surrounded by four large pontoons that kept the tank afloat in the Willamette River. The tank was made of slats, four inches wide, placed about an inch apart on the bottom and about two inches apart on the sides, allowing constant change of water. It was loads of fun swimming in the Willamette River but, alas, the evil of pollution was to bring it to an end.

Portland: Council Crest Amusement Park. A twenty-minute ride by trolley car, over a winding and scenic route, lands you 1,200 feet above the city. From Council Crest thousands of tourists have said the view is beyond compare — the mountains in the distance, the scenery of the Columbia and Willamette rivers, and the joy of looking down on the City of Portland. The area was an amusement park until 1929, when the city took it over as a scenic park. All the concessions were removed, as they were presenting problems for surrounding residential areas. (Bottom) The entrance to the amusement park. The track of the scenic railway can be seen in the background. (Top) Closeup of some of the concessions, the scenic railway, miniature railway, and "Trip up the Columbia." The latter would appear from the outside to be a ride on one of the stern-wheelers. Inside the large riverboat you boarded a small rowboat-sized vessel for an "old mill" type of water trip covering two or three blocks.

(Above upper) The famous *Portland Hotel* was started in 1883, the same year the transcontinental *Northern Pacific Railway* arrived in Portland over the *Oregon Railway & Navigation Company* tracks. Henry Villard, president of the NP and ORN, saw the importance of having a choice hotel to accommodate the many people who would now be coming west. He hired the famous New York architect, Stanford White, along with others, to draw plans for this establishment. In 1884 financial troubles caught up with Villard, and work on the hotel was stopped. Local financing took over the operation, and the hotel was opened in 1890, representing an investment of about one million dollars. Meier & Frank Company bought the hotel in 1944, and it was dismantled in 1952. (Above lower) The spacious dining room of the *Portland Hotel*.

The Portland Rose Festival: For You A Rose In Portland Grows. "The Portland Rose Festival is a Mardi Gras of flowers, whose beauty and poetic grandeur have eclipsed every carnival of the nation and challenged the admiration of the civilized world." The Portland Rose Society held its first show in a tent in 1889. The Rose Festival as we know it today began in 1907; the first parade was a "horse-and-buggy show." Portland Rose parade scenes taken between 1905 and 1910. (Above) One of the very early scenes of the festival. Photo was taken on what today would be the Stadium grounds. The old Multnomah Club can be seen in background. (Below) This float of Portland Fire Department Truck No. 4 won the first prize trophy for 1908.

(Above) Portland school children marched in what was called "Rosebud" parade. Photo was taken on Grand Avenue on East Side of Portland. (Below) The parade is shown on Morrison Street looking east between Ninth and Tenth streets. Note bleachers erected for the early festivals.

Lewis and Clark Centennial Exposition and Oriental Fair Portland 1905: Probably nothing ever achieved brought the attention of Portland and the state of Oregon before the world like the Lewis and Clark Fair. The fair was just reasonably attended by our Eastern cousins, but word got back of our beautiful surroundings, delightful climate, and a better and more wholesome way of living. The next few years saw Oregon's greatest growth. Above is the Agricultural Palace and a rest area at the fair.

(Above) A view from the Agricultural Palace. U.S. Government Building on the man-built island in Guilds Lake has a full frontage of 1,025 feet. Bridge of Nations connects the Government Building with the main area. In center can be seen the popular bandstand, where visitors are entertained daily. The Esplanade is the avenue of travel between the bandstand and the Bridge of Nations.

(Right) Sight-seeing on Lewis and Clark Avenue, a street named after the early Oregon explorers. The lady is raising her skirt to keep it dry. This photo may have been taken a short time after one of Oregon's showers. The two people carrying umbrellas almost confirm this. These people have learned that rain makes Oregon wealthy, healthy, and green. Buildings shown, left to right: Oriental, European, and Agricultural.

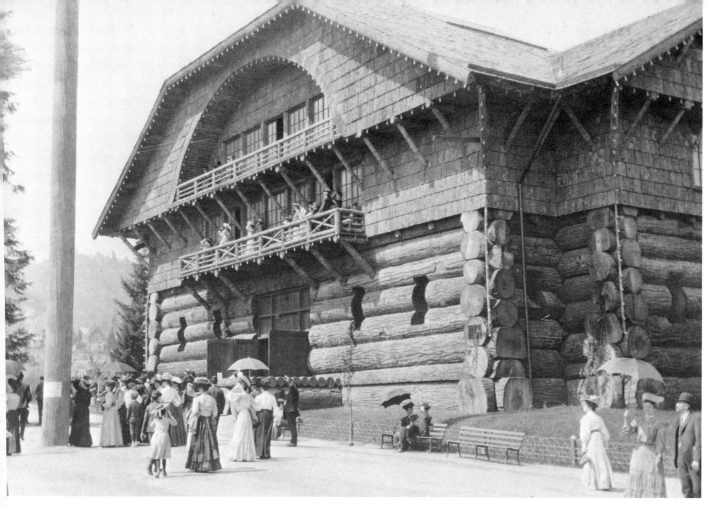

(Above) Forestry Building — the largest log cabin in the world. The Forestry Building was constructed of great unhewn logs. The building was 100 feet wide and 200 feet long and was a popular place on the grounds. It was one of the few buildings retained after the fair closed. It burned in 1964. Ladies have their umbrellas up to protect them from the Oregon sun.

(Above) A milk ranch of 1890 located in the Marquam Hill area. A man can be seen carrying a bucket of milk from the barn, while the chickens can be seen behind. The Chick Sale outhouse is centrally located between the house and barn, with the well on a higher area directly in front of the home.

(Left) Balderree family goes for a Sunday afternoon ride in their 1913 Overland to the restful Portland west hills. Either the car is overheated and needs to cool, or our lady is thirsty and wants a springwater drink. These troughs or drinking spots were located every mile or so for horses pulling heavy loads over the old dusty road.

Whose job was it to keep the stove hot? Flashlight Photo Company, 203½ First Street, Portland, 1910. (Left to right) Anna Pope Linquist, Wilfred Bicknell, Maude Pope Allyn.

It is believed this is Jacob Benjamin Neubauer, an early Portland grocer who for many years served the West Side area. Note gas light, coffee grinder, string holder, and bread case.

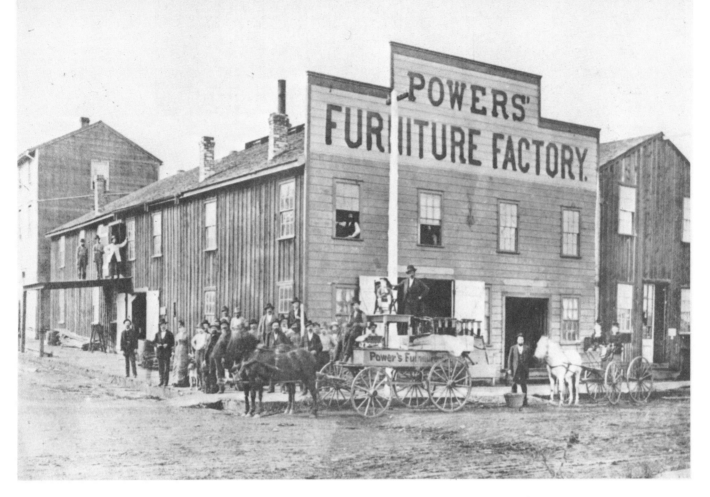

Portland about 1877: Power's Furniture Factory located at Jefferson and Front streets.

Three women in high button shoes are drinking from one of the twenty bronze fountains donated by the lumber king, Simon Benson, to the city of Portland in 1912. Old Portland Hotel can be seen in background.

Portland 1902: The first unit of the Ford Street Bridge, completed in 1903 and now replaced by the Vista Avenue Bridge. It was in use for some ten years. Note Canyon Road beneath bridge. Robert Wynne Wilson, who as a boy crossed the Ford Street Bridge en route to school at Portland Academy, tells us when the Council Crest and Portland Heights trolley cars crossed over the bridge the wooden planking gave a rumbling and cracking sound.

Portland 1895: Bishop Scott Academy. This was a boarding school for boys located on S.W. Eighteenth between Couch and Everett streets. The school was in operation from about 1870 to 1904. In the back row of students is George Willis Wilson. Some of the officers are Cap Young, Charles Canby, and Sidney K. Hooper.

Portland July 4, 1911 (Montavilla Parade). The parked automobile is a 1911 Apperson, while the first two cars in the parade are a 1911 Chalmers-Detroit and a 1911 Franklin.

The George F. Sanborn home, built in 1910, located at the northwest corner of Twenty-fifth and Marshall streets. The automobile is a 1913 Model T Ford.

Portland about 1900: Looking east down Marquam gulch. Ross Island can be seen in the middle of the Willamette River. The trestle in the foreground, now Barbur Boulevard, is the *Southern Pacific's* trackage up Fourth Avenue and out to Beaverton and Hillsboro (the old *Oregon Central Railroad)*. The trestle in the background offers some discussion but is believed to be the *Portland & Willamette Valley Railroad* trackage from the Jefferson Street levee to Oswego. Marquam gulch was at that time the city dump. Portions west of Fourth Street trestle were made into Duniway Park in 1925.

Portland 1915: Looking north on Fifth Avenue. Cross street is Taylor. Photo shows two large private homes, each occupying a full block and located in the center of the city. (Left) *Failing Home:* Built approximately 1876 and torn down in early 1920s. It was the last residence of Henrietta Ellison Failing and Mary Forbush Failing, daughters of Henry Failing, who died in 1898. The Public Service Building has been at this location since 1927. (Right) *Corbett Home:* Built in 1875 and torn down in 1936. It was the last residence of Mrs. Henry Winslow (Emma L. Ruggles) Corbett. Corbett died in 1903, but his widow continued to live in the seventeen-room mansion. In 1917 her cow made news nationally when a writer for *Collier's* magazine wrote a feature on Portland and cited "The Million Dollar Cow Pasture." Today the Pacific Building and the stage terminal utilize the space.

Silas Christofferson, Oregon's Edison of the air, made a spectacular flight on June 11, 1912, from the roof of the Multnomah Hotel to Pearson Field in Vancouver, Washington. The flight took twelve minutes in his forty-horsepower plane. Photo shows plane over Pacific Paper Company located at Fourth and Ankeny streets.

Home of John Wilson, located at the corner of Fourteenth and Taylor streets in 1870. At the time the home was built it was Twelfth Street, but this was changed to Fourteenth Street about the turn of the century.

Portland 1895: *Portland Cable Railway,* built in 1890 and in existence only a few years, was constructed to promote home building on Portland Heights. The cable line took off south of Eighteenth Street* near Market Street, then up the hill to Spring Street (about 500 feet altitude). A powerhouse was constructed on Eighteenth Street near Mill Street. The cable line, never a financial success, made it easy for those not interested in riding the cable cars by constructing a walk up the steep incline with a railed broadwalk suspended a little below the car track. Though the cable car was of short duration, the promotion did help the growth of Portland Heights.

---

*Eighteenth Street at that time was known as Chapman Street.

Olds & King dry goods department in 1898. Store was originally started by John Wilson and sold in 1879 to Olds & King. (Left) First man is Robert Wynne Wilson; fourth man is Mr. Goudy. Note all male clerks.

Frame house of Capt. Nathaniel Crosby, S.W. First and Washington streets, built in 1847. He was the late Bing Crosby's great-grandfather. Later it became the home of the *Oregon Native Son*, an early historical publication.

Portland 1894: Flood. Fireboat No. 1 of the Portland Fire Department is shown on First Avenue (Chinatown section) in June 1894 during the record high water. A fire engine was placed on a barge to pump water in case of fires in the flooded areas.

Portland Police in their 1913 Pope Hartford automobile. In front seat is Capt. John T. Moore, battalion commander; standing is Sergeant Rupert, battalion adjutant. Others unknown.

Portland 1913: Front view of the new police station at Second and Oak streets which included a jail and courtroom. Vehicles shown (left to right) 1911 Pope Hartford paddy wagon, 1913 White, 1913 Pope Hartford. Some of the police officers shown are Chief John Clark, Capt. John T. Moore, and Capt. Harry A. Circle. The plainclothesman is believed to be Capt. C. E. Baty, head of detectives. Some of the other officers shown are F. R. Gouldstone, A. O. Abbott, E. G. Marsh, and possibly J. Burri or R. A. Mainwaring. In 1912 speeding became such a problem that the Portland *Oregonian* listed, sometimes on the front page much like a box score, those who exceeded the fifteen-mile-an-hour limit. This often included some of the most important people in Portland. The fines were usually $20 to $30 each. Automobiles at that date were not equipped with speedometers, but the judge would not accept this excuse. (If you had a speedometer on your car it was extra equipment added at the time of purchase.)

Portland 1906: Progress for the fire department! Mike Laudenklos, assistant chief (left), working directly under Chief David Campbell, replaces his horse-drawn buggy with a new 1906 Model N Ford. Batt. Chief Frank ("Biddy") Dowell, captain of Truck Company No. 1 (right), is also shown. (Dowell was later appointed chief of Portland Fire Department from 1911 to 1920.) New Ford comes without windshield and has right-hand drive. Photo taken at Portland City Hall, located between Fourth and Fifth, and Madison and Jefferson streets.

Bailey Gatzert on the Willamette River showing Portland in the background. There were many of these steamboat-sternwheelers running between Portland-Astoria and The Dalles.

Early Portland water scene, with a windjammer tied up at the dock along the Willamette River. The *W. S. Mason* ferry operated to Albina and can be seen crossing the river. At that time the Albina area consisted of the *Northern Pacific Terminal Company* yards and the dry dock of *Oregon Railway & Navigation Company*. The ferry was named after a former mayor, William S. Mason, who was instrumental in annexing Albina as a part of Portland. The ferry ceased operations with completion of the Broadway Bridge.

(Left) 1910: The ferry *City of Vancouver* ran between Vancouver, Washington, and Hayden Island (Portland) from 1909 to 1917 until it was replaced by the Interstate Highway Bridge between the two states. (Railroad bridge can be seen in the background.)

(Below) 1885: Stark Street ferry was one of the principal means of crossing the Willamette River. Wagonload of cordwood to be used for fuel is being moved from East Portland to Portland. The first talk of a bridge across the river brought opposition. As might be expected, Jack and Levi Knott, operators of the Stark Street ferry did not like the idea; neither did shipping interests and waterfront property owners. Their difference of opinion resulted in court action. An injunction was obtained, but not until the case reached the U.S. Supreme Court did Portland's first bridge get the go-ahead signal. The Morrison Bridge was opened April 13, 1887. The historic river ferry will entirely disappear from Oregon waters very soon. Oregon became a state in 1859, and since then dozens of these ferries have been replaced by new bridges. In 1959 there were eight ferries in the state; by 1976 there were only four, three on the Willamette River and one on the Columbia River.

City & Suburban Railway Company carbarns at S.E. Twenty-Sixth and Powell Streets in 1891, with a crew of motormen and conductors in front of one of Portland's latest trolley cars. The man sitting down puffing the cigar must be either the senior motorman or the trainmaster.

They prepare restful beds on the train and make sweet music on their day off. Sleeping car Pullman porters pose for their picture behind the tailgate of Union Pacific's *Portland Limited*.

Observation Car "Seeing Portland." The traction company had several of these observation cars, and they were very popular among visitors. For 50¢ you would be taken to the top of Council Crest, over the bridge to the East Side, downtown, and into some of the better residential areas. It was a good way to see the city. (Above) about 1915: This trip was a businessmen's tour and was under the direct supervision of Frank Darius Hunt, man standing on the ground. (Mr. Hunt was Traffic Manager for the *Portland Railway Light & Power Company* and later president of the *Willamette Valley Southern Railway*.)

Portland 1913: A. J. Winters Company of Sixth Street. A. J. Winters is driving the 1913 Pope Hartford automobile; M. Winters can be seen on top of tires.

Oregon Railway & Navigation Company (Union Pacific) diner on the Chicago-Portland Special of 1905: Note transom grill and leaded glass above windows and hand-done decor on vaulted ceiling panels.

(Far right): Oregon Taxi Cab Company had fifteen of these 1912 Fiat Townsedans for use in Portland. Note cab driver's uniform with "O.T." on his cap. Taxi is stopped in front of Imperial Hotel on S.W. Broadway, corner of Stark. Hotel Oregon, shown on opposite corner, has been dismantled; Trader Vic's is in the location today. Other half of building extending to S.W. Oak now houses the Benson Hotel. Across from hotel is Commerce Building.

Ezra Royce, who operated a Portland cab service, owned this 1914 Franklin Town Car. Photo taken in the 400 block on West Park, Portland. We tired to secure the name of the brick building with marquee but never succeeded. Can you help?

This 1907 six-cylinder Model K Ford was one of only a few hundred such cars built by Henry Ford. He attempted to enter the larger car field but apparently considered the small car better suited to his market. This particular car was purchased by *Southern Pacific Company,* flange wheels were added, and it was used for inspection work on many of the Oregon branch lines. Note SP emblem on door.

Two Southern Pacific officials, Frank L. Burchhalter and H. A. Hinshaw, touring the area in a four-cylinder 1912 KRIT.

Fourteen-passenger Detroit electric bus in front of the Imperial Hotel. Bus met all incoming trains. If you registered at the hotel, the bus would carry you free of charge from the railroad station. During off hours it often made short trips around town to accommodate guests, who were charged 25¢. Note hard tires, chain drive, and open windshield. On opposite corner can be seen American Express Agency.

The Portland street car system had its first serious run-in with the automobile in 1915 in the form of jitneys. These unregulated and privately operated automobiles cruised along the trolley lines, skimming off transit business. A city election, followed by a city ordinance, brought this menace to an end. Clyde Catching can be seen in front of his privately owned jitney that competed with the St. Johns streetcars.

A 1913 Stutz Bearcat photographed in the Park blocks and driven by Frank E. Watkins. Two of the churches shown are still in use today: (left) St. James Lutheran; (right) First Congregational Church. Note bandstand so popular a few years ago.

Portland 1927: Broadway looking south from Oak Street. Marquee over the center of the street reads Liberty Theatre. On the opposite page it has been changed to Music Box. Benson Hotel can be seen on right corner. One block south on Stark Street on the north corner is United States National Bank, while on the south corner is Imperial Hotel.

1909 or 1910 EMF opera coupe on display at EMF office, corner Alder and Chapman streets, Portland. Mr. Everett, Mr. Metzger and Mr. Flanders formed a company in 1908 to manufacture automobiles. The Flanders was a small car, the Everett was a medium-sized car, and the "EMF" was a large car. In 1913 they consolidated with the Studebaker Automobile Company. The public jokingly referred to these cars as "Every Morning Fixem."

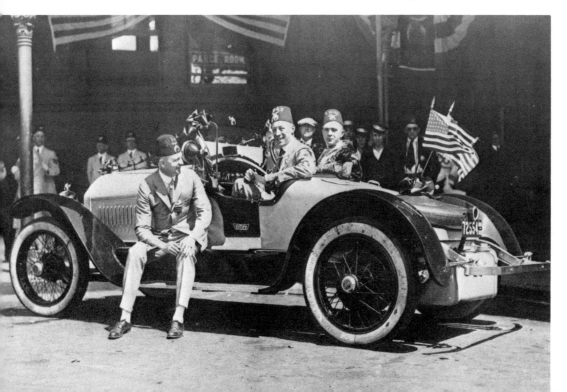

National Shrine Convention held in Portland in June 1920. Three Shriners in 1920 Stutz roadster (left to right) Leslie French, Imperial Potentate William Freeland Kendrick, and Frank E. Watkins. Photo taken in front of Union Station.

Portland 1928-29: Broadway at night, looking south from Stark Street. (Left) Music Box advertises "talking pictures." This was the period when silent films were on their way out. Many of the smaller theaters could not afford the $6,000 to $7,000 needed to convert to sound. For a year or so a theater with a sign "Talking Pictures" might show only one reel of talkies, while the feature would be a silent movie. The changeover from silents to talkies found Hollywood unprepared. Many small neighborhood theaters, unable to meet the expense of conversion, saw attendance drop off at a rapid rate as talkies caught on.

Portland about 1910: Third Avenue looking north. Cross street is Alder. At the extreme left is the Masonic Temple Building, used from 1871 to 1920s with the ground floor occupied by J. K. Gill Company from 1892 to 1921.

Portland 1924: Looking north on Fifth Avenue, corner of Morrison Street. Note policeman directing traffic. Automobiles shown (left to right in front): 1924 Hupmobile, 1922 Packard, 1923 Model T Ford roadster (rear end only).

Portland 1911: Looking north on Sixth Avenue between Yamhill and Morrison streets. (Left side of street): Hotel Portland, with Frank Nau drugstore on Morrison corner. Marquam Building opposite corner; Marquam Rooming House; the Oregonian Building with its massive tower (corner of Alder Street). (Right side of street): Stearns Building, occupied by Sherman & Clay music store and Charles F. Berg's store. (Today Meier & Frank Company has the full block.) All these buildings have been torn down and replaced. Automobile to the left is 1910 White Steam Car.

Portland 1925: Looking West on Washington Street at Fifth. Note policeman in middle of street. The automobile in the center is a 1919 Dodge. On the extreme right is a 1923 Dodge. Dodge Brothers from 1908 to 1915 manufactured most of the mechanical parts for the Ford automobile. In 1915 Dodge discontinued this arrangement and started producing a car of its own.

Portland 1911: Sixth and Stark streets. Reo 1911 car in left corner.

Broadway and Washington streets in 1914, the most important corner in the city. Horse-drawn bus is shown in front of
the Imperial Hotel. These buses met all incoming trains.
Some of the automobiles shown are (left to right) 1909 Oldsmobile Limited, 1909 four-cylinder Franklin, 1913
Studebaker.

Portland 1913: Stark Street looking west between Fourth and Fifth avenues. (Center): Delivering ice in an open-end wagon — this was big business throughout the city before the coming of electric and gas refrigerators. First three automobiles shown (left to right): 1912 Overland, 1909 Pierce, 1911 Oakland.

"Here Comes the Wells Fargo Wagon!" The Wells Fargo Company opened an office in 1852 on Front Street. In 1874 the company moved to the Annex of the New Market Building on the corner of Ankeny and First streets and remained there until the flood of 1894. The last headquarters was at Fifth and Hoyt streets, shown below.

Portland Union Station (left): Note buses and Council Crest streetcar awaiting arrival of incoming trains.

Sixth and Stark street about 1914. Imperial Hotel is on the left.

COASTAL AREA

At the base of *Neahkahnie Mountain* 1913 (Tillamook County): The bark *Glenesslin* on the rocks. She was an English bark from Northampton. The vessel was broken up by the pounding sea.

North Bend August 24, 1916: The Railroad Jubilee celebrated the opening of the rail line from valley points to the Coos Bay area. Dignitaries from all over the state attended, including Gov. James Withycombe from Salem. (Above) Southern Pacific all-Pullman train can be seen with Coos Bay waterway in the background. The Royal Rosarians in white uniforms, with Bandmaster Charles Kaiser, can be seen marching on Sherman Avenue.

Local talent auto racers performed with their Model T Ford Bugs of 1912-14-15 vintage. Shown are (left to right) Vern Gorst, flagman; man standing on ground between second and third car is Horace Byler, policeman between third and fourth cars is C. J. Anderson. Percy Phillip won the twenty-five mile race; I. R. Tower came in third.

Coos Bay (Coos County): "The Treasure Chest of Oregon." At the time this photo was taken the city was called Marshfield, a name used for some ninety years but changed in 1944 to Coos Bay. (Above) 1910: Front Street business establishments. (Left) Preuss Drug Store and Blanco Hotel, corner of Commercial Avenue; the Central Hotel and Flanagan and Bennett Bank at Market Street; (Right) Butler Building. Some of the occupants were Dr. William Horsfall and Dr. Prentis, Dentist.

Coos Bay 1914: Steamer *Breakwater*, owned by Southern Pacific Company and sailing between Portland and Coos Bay, has delivered the first shipment of 1914 Model T Fords to the Tower Motor Company, still in business today. Steamer service handling both freight and passenger traffic was used before the rail line was constructed into Coos Bay.

89

People Viewing
Santa Clara

(Left) *Coos Bay* 1895 (Coos County): Barkentine Arago, lumber schooner, loaded and ready to depart. *Coos Bay, Roseburg & Eastern Railroad & Navigation Company* locomotive pulling out empty flat car after transferring its lading to the *Arago*. (CBR&EN No. 2 is 4-4-0 class locomotive built by Cuyahoga in 1872.)

Wheeler 1912 (Tillamook County): Southern Pacific McKeen Gas Motor Coach No. 41 arrives en route to Tillamook. These cars were often referred to as "skunks," as they burned gasoline for their operation. The white building directly behind the McKeen car was the Wheeler Hotel; the same building today is the Rinehart Clinic.

(Left) *Entrance to Coos Bay,* November 1915: *Santa Clara,* on the Portland to San Francisco run, went aground on the South Spit near the entrance to Coos Bay Harbor. Two small boats capsized in the heavy seas, resulting in the loss of sixteen people. Photo shows the scene the following day, with a 1909 Packard automobile on the beach.

Mohler 1912 (Tillamook County): The town, named after a Union Pacific Railroad official, came into existence with the building of the *Pacific Railway & Navigation Company*. Henry Tohl had operated a general merchandise store in Nehalem and decided to open a similar store in Mohler, with railroad serve now available. Shown in photo are Henry Tohl, standing in the front door; Alva Finley, the local manager, standing beside Tohl; "Grandpa" Fred Rabitech, seated man with whiskers; Augusta Wist, lady with checkered dress. Others are from nearby homes.

(Left) *Timber* (Washington County): This was once an important railroad town, where helper locomotives were added to each passing train to give them power enough to get over the hill. Many trainmen who worked in the roundhouse and on the locomotives lived in Timber and supported the merchants. Today big diesels, pulling long freight trains, highball through the town and up over the hill. As a result trainmen have moved away, and the town has suffered a decline.

(Above) *Watseco* 1913 (Tillamook County): Oregon is the timber state of the nation. The cedar tree shown is fifty-three feet in circumference. It is one of the "toothpicks" raised in this state. (Left to right) Nellie Shand Watt, George Shand, Helen Shand, Margaret Wilhelmina (Watt) Edwards, George Watt. (The Watt family were successful lumber operators in Tillamook County.)

A 1912 Flanders making a trip along Yaquina Bay. The trip followed the coastline. It would appear they were having road trouble. (Left to right) J. D. Grant, driver; Will Burton, organizer of trip; T. F. Kershaw, editor of the *Newport Signal*.

(Left) *Salmonberry Station* 1911 (Tillamook County): A fisherman's paradise near Timber, Oregon. *Pacific Railway & Navigation Company* mixed train carrying excursionists to picnic and fish in the Salmonberry River, a delightful area and stream located in the Coast Range. A mixed train is one carrying both freight and passenger cars. Note white flags on the pilot of the locomotive. This indicates train is running as a "special" and is not governed by the timetable. Note new ties without ballast. This would indicate track has just been laid. PRN No. 1 is 4-4-0 wood-burner locomotive built in 1880.)

Neskowin 1890 (Tillamook County): Boat in Slab Creek with Proposal Rock in background. (Left to right) man standing in the bow, Harry Hayes Stapleton; girl with feet in the water, Anna Golden; little boy in front, Roy Stapleton; two girls in front with hat, Collins girls; girl standing in front, Agnes Gilbert Schucking; little girl in extreme rear, Jennie Fry Walsh; two boys in back, Richardson boys. Three people sitting in water: (Left to right) Belle Golden Steiner, George Collins, Ada Stapleton Baumgartner.

During World War I *Alsea Southern Railroad No. 12,* a twenty-three-mile rail line, was constructed from the south side of Yaquina Bay (South Beach) to Alsea Bay. This line was built by the U.S. Government Spruce Division Railroad as a way to remove some of the large stands of spruce trees so important for airplane construction. After the war there was no need for the trackage. The only usable highway between South Beach and Waldport traveled along the ocean front, pretty much on the beach. As automobiles became more plentiful, a beach highway was not satisfactory for auto traffic. A 1919 Model T Ford was equipped with flange wheels to operate this distance over the sixty-pound rail. Here is the Model T Ford en route to Waldport about 1920.

Siletz about 1910 (Lincoln County): Indians of the area have their own celebration for a holiday memorial.

Astoria 1904: Finnish Brotherhood Lodge funeral.

(Above) *T. J. Potter* leaving Astoria in 1905 heading for Portland. The *T. J. Potter* carried both passengers and freight and was one of the fastest boats on the river.

A 1911 parade celebrates the founding of Astoria. Automobile to right is a one-cylinder Brush. Note wooden streets; much of the town at that period was built on piling.

Washington Irving was the lion among American literati. .

Astoria, located at the mouth of the Columbia River, was the first city founded by Americans west of the Mississippi River. John Jacob Astor's fur-trading party arrived here March 22, 1811, on the ship *Tonquin*. The city was well known by name long before many larger cities along the West Coast. Much of the credit goes to Washington Irving (1783-1859) who wrote the book *Astoria*, first published in 1837. One hundred and twenty editions have been printed.

A portion of Astoria, showing its brewery along the waterfront in 1910. Note the electric streetcar of the *Astoria Street Railway* covering the waterfront area. A dray is being pulled from the beer distributor for the town's use.

Newport 1894: A Salem group dressed almost formally enjoy the summer beach air of the Pacific Ocean. Man eating on left, Harry David ("Hal") Patton; lady in rear, Jessie Breyman McNary (wife of U.S. Sen. Charles Linza McNary); lady in center, Ada Stapleton Baumgartner; man and woman on right end, George Francis Rodgers and Blanche Albert Rodgers.

Peter Healy, Newport postmaster, and companion near the south jetty trestle located at the entrance of the harbor.

Newport 1912: The biggest event of the day was the evening arrival of the steamship *Newport*. The Corvallis & Eastern Railroad terminated at Yaquina City, where train passengers transferred to the boat for a three-mile trip across Yaquina Bay to the city of Newport. The entire town turned out to see who was arriving. Horse-drawn buses carried guests to their particular hotel. Ladies on balcony (right) were Abbey Hotel chambermaids. They, too, stopped work to watch the arrival of tourists and visitors from the valley.

Helen Pearce, Dorothy Pearce, and Clifford Arthur Brasfield enjoy the Newport beach in 1907. Helen Pearce later became a doctor of philosophy and was head of Willamette University's English department for some seventeen years.

Cathryn Lindsay enjoys the beach air in a 1923 sport roadster Model T Ford. Note extras on the car — spotlight, side wings, and especially the nice-looking gal.

Rockaway: One of the Tillamook beaches and a big favorite with Oregon folks. (Left) 1916: The daily passenger train with open-end observation car leaves for Portland. The entire town turns out to see whose vacation is over and who must return to his job the next morning. (Note tents along the track; today this is part of the highway system.) Only one person can be identified. The small newsboy standing beside the track is Charles Raymon Lindsay, who still lives in Rockaway.

Rockaway 1921 or 1922 (Tillamook County): Southern Pacific passenger train No. 141 just arrived from Portland. Plank road will eventually be U.S. Highway 101. Railroad station with outside plumbing can be seen in background. Pacific Ocean can also be seen. SP-2926 (4-8-0) Cooke engine built in 1882. Locomotive has "new tires." Automobiles shown (left to right): 1919 Model T Ford, 1919 Chandler, 1912 Hudson, 1919 Model T Ford (back end only).

Neahkahnie Mountain is located a few miles north of two Oregon coastal towns, Nehalem and Manzanita, in Tillamook County. The mountain offers a breath-taking, unobstructed view of the Pacific Ocean. The rock-formation mountain, some 1,800 feet high, is a spur of the Coast Range that jets out into the sea. The wide expanse of the restless Pacific stretches to right and left and far ahead. This modern picture of U.S. Highway 101 after its opening in 1941 shows how they blasted a shelf out of the face of the cliff some 300 feet above the water. (Photo at bottom of page 103 shows how the highway looked in an earlier time.)

Astoria has had its share of fires over the years. Firemen in 1885 had to be endurance men and good runners. Shown is Rescue Hose Company No. 2 ready to leave on an emergency call. Note wooden sidewalks and planked road. Building shown in center rear is old St. Mary's Hospital.

Large mounds of shells were left in Seaside, discarded by the Clatsop Indians who lived here many years before. The city of Seaside, years after the Indians departed, crushed these shells into a sandlike substance. This was ideal for a path or substitute sidewalk and was used between Pool's Bowling Alley (Downing Street today) and the promenade along the ocean. It was known as the Shell Road and today is a part of Broadway Street.

Fort Stevens (Clatsop County): During the Civil War the U.S. Army became concerned for the fortification of the mouth of the Columbia River. They worried about Emperor Maximilian in Mexico and the danger of Confederate cruisers preying on Union ships in the Pacific. The fort was completed in 1865 and actually had been under discussion as a project since 1820. These defenses finally came into being as a result of the Civil War. The last of the first big guns were removed in 1901 to make way for concrete emplacements for six-inch rifles. Battery Russell, built later, was completed in 1904. The entire fort was abandoned by the U.S. military in 1947. (Above) 1910 photo shows the U.S. barracks and military personnel necessary to man the fort. Man with "X" is John Ellis Graham. (Below) 1910 view shows Battery Russell, named after Gen. David A. Russell, who had been killed in action during the Civil War.

Going to the beach was loads of fun, but it was also nice to hear from your friends back home. The U.S. mail did a thriving postcard and letter business. Before the coming of the *Astoria & Columbia River Railroad* in 1898, mail for seaside was handled by steamboat to Astoria or Warrenton, thence via *Astoria & South Coast Railroad* or stage line to Seaside.

Gearhart 1911 (Clatsop County): This beautiful hotel overlooking the Pacific Ocean was built by Theodore Kruse and partners. The hotel advertised "Golf links, Natatorium and Automobiling." Kruse had a restaurant background, as he was already operating the Louvre restaurant in Portland. Before selling his Gearhart Hotel in 1913 he made a wager with some of his cronies that any amount received over $100,000 would be spent towards a party for all his friends. The hotel sold for $103,000, and Theo put on a party at the Louvre that will long be remembered in Portland. (Above) The Gearhart Hotel from the beach side.

SOUTHERN OREGON

Oregon Caves National Monument in Josephine County is located some 50 miles due south of Grants Pass. Homer D. Harkness and Walter C. Burch of Leland, Oregon located the caves in 1885 and constructed a cabin and camping accommodation for tourists. The area was proclaimed a National Monument in 1909. In this picture the Oregon Caves Stage (a 1917 Oldsmobile) is shown with Charles W. Stinger at the extreme left, lower level. At the upper level can be seen the entrance to the caves. The man on the far right is Richard W. Rowley, Ranger-in-Charge and official guide for many years.

The border between *Oregon* and *California;* The automobile is a 1921 Page.

Ashland 1935: Abandoned Chautauqua bowl often used for various plays. This photo was taken just prior to the opening of the first Oregon Shakespearean Festival season July 4, 1935, according to Angus Bowmar, festival founder. The festival's first stagehouse had been erected and the grounds were being prepared for the benches (lower left) soon to be installed.

Odell Lake 1925 (Klamath County): Guests in front of the Odell Lodge.

Klamath Falls 1913: This odd-looking tent contraption was used by the City to keep their streets clean of debris. The driver was Charlie Adams, and the photo was taken at Sixth and Oak streets.

Medford (Jackson County): "The new town in the Rogue River Valley, which is to be the railroad shipping point for Jacksonville, is called Medford. It displays symptoms of future growth." *(West Shore* magazine 1884) "Medford would never have existed but for the shortsightedness of the citizens of Jacksonville, for had they paid a subsidy to the builders of the *Oregon & California Railroad* of a paltry $2,500, the railroad would be passing through Jacksonville today." (Left) about 1910: Main Street, at that time unpaved. Automobile to the left is a two-cylinder 1908 Maxwell. (Above) Same street a few years later as the "gas buggies" become more noticeable. SP-2347 (4-6-0) Baldwin locomotive built in 1911.

In order to reach Klamath Falls, before the coming of the Southern Pacific in May 1909, one boarded the *Klamath Lake Railroad,* at Thrall, California, located on the main line of the SP, and rode to Pokegame, Oregon, located in the Cascade Mountains. At this point you transferred to a stage for a ride to Keno, Oregon, and then boarded the steamboat *Klamath* for a ride up the Klamath River and across Lake Ewauna to the city of Klamath Falls. After the arrival of the railroad the steamer *Klamath* was no longer needed to serve the Lower Lake area. In 1910 the boat was moved by rail to the Upper Lake area. Photo shows spectators in the Lakeside Inn hack watching the slightly unorthodox moving of the *Klamath* over the railroad on a flatcar.

Near *Trail* 1925 (Jackson County): The Rogue Elk Hotel
shown in photo is a stop-off point for those en route to Crater
Lake. Hotels of this class have been replaced today by motels.
Automobile under the arch is 1923 Chevrolet.

Klamath Falls 1912: Linkville trolley running east on Main Street at intersection of Fourth. Hall Hotel can be seen in background (now the Stevens). Charlie Adams drove the old trolley, pulled by two horses.

Roseburg August 22, 1912: Grand Hotel lobby, with Mr. and Mrs. Fred Schwartz behind the counter.

Roseburg 1911 (Douglas County): Sheridan Street looking east, with the intersection of Pine Street shown in photo. The blast of 1959 destroyed almost all these buildings. Building to the right reading "drugs" housed The Maccabees, with a drugstore on the ground floor.

Pelican Bay or *Harriman Lodge* (Klamath County): Edward Henry Harriman, Union Pacific Railroad executive and financier, spent the summer of 1907 here attempting to regain his health. He was told that the southern Oregon air and sparkling water made this the ideal spot for recreation and rest. Harriman lived only two years longer. Shown is one of the groups stopping here.

(Left opposite page) *Crater Lake* 1917 — Rim Village Area: Crater Lake Lodge, a picturesque inn built in 1914 and constructed mainly of the gray stone of the region, occupies a noble site on the very rim of the lake, some 1,000 feet below. The two automobiles are (left to right) a 1914 Peerless and a 1916 Oakland.

Crater Lake July 1916: E. B. Hall and family enjoy the snow in their 1914 Franklin.

Arrow: A 1914 view of Larry Gorman's new home on homestead land in southeast Lake County, where the population is shown as twenty-five people.

Klamath Agency 1927 (Klamath County): Capt. Oliver Cromwell Applegate meets with Klamath Indians — Captain Sky and family.

Fort Klamath 1914 (Klamath County): A 1913 Metz automobile crossing the Wood River Bridge.

Oakland July 4, 1910 (Douglas County): The Fourth of July parade. Some of those participating are W. C. Underwood, Charles L. and Pitzer W. Beckley, Alva Wise, Mr. and Mrs. Lynn Caton, James H. Dearling, C. A. Pengra, J. Henderson Miller, Harmon A. Collins, Edward W. Brooks, Frank W. Hunt, and Fred J. Blakeley.

Prospect 1915 (Jackson County): James E. Grieve, postmaster and owner of the general merchandise store is shown on left. His wife, in center of picture, helps with the store and also acts as manager of the Prospect Hotel (right).

Galice (Josephine County): A small mining town in southern Oregon that produced some five million dollars in gold dust. This area was one of many such mines in Josephine County. (Above) Scene taken about 1900 shows packtrain leaving town after making the necessary purchases at J. E. Loomis's General Store. The only town official was E. S. Merrill, justice of the peace.

Stephen Hall Meek (1807-1886): Came to Oregon in 1835; mountain guide and trapper. He was responsible for the lost wagon train of 1845. He used a short-cut instead of following the well-marked Oregon Trail, and the party became hopelessly lost. He escaped being hanged by his own party by stealing away at night. Stephen was brother to Oregon's famous Joe Meek.

Boswell Springs about 1890 (Douglas County): The springs were named after Captain Boswell, a veteran of the Mexican War. The hotel, located in the Yoncalla Valley, was noted for fine meals as well as for the curative benefits of baths in the mineral water. The big hotel burned about 1901-1902. SP-1253 Baldwin (4-4-0).

J. W. Kelsey and his 1920 Harley Davidson motorcycle (note chains on the back wheel).

WILLAMETTE VALLEY

Coalca 1920 (Clackamas County): A station on the Southern Pacific located about halfway between Oregon City and Canby. The name is used as a location mark for trainmen serving (left) the Doernbecker sawmill, today called Samuel's Lumber Company. Note stern-wheeler in the middle of the Willamette River opposite Rock Island. (Right) Coalca's Pillar (sometimes called Balancing Rock) is a natural formation located at the top of the hill. Tiny Christmas tree thrives in a most unlikely home, for the rock is at least fifteen feet high. Indian legend has it that Chief Coalca was disappointed in love and took his life by leaping from the rock.

Looking south through Southern Pacific's covered railroad bridge crossing the Clackamas River on the main line to California in 1890. Park Place School and Abernathy Heights can be seen to left. The ferry (right) was available in case the railroad bridge washed out, collapsed, or burned. People shown are (left to right) Freddie Cross, Mrs. Truman (Ollie) Cross, Truman Cross (on horse), Fred Cross and David D. Cross (on handcar), Frankie Cross, Dell Cross (who ran the ferry), Louis Himler, John Griner. Cross Park occupies the same area today.

A 1940 crossing of the Clackamas River at about the same location as above. Shown is Southern Pacific's deluxe passenger train, *The Cascade*, pulled by a 4300 mountain-type locomotive (4-8-2). The Clackamas River became well known when Rudyard Kipling, then more of a newspaperman than a novelist, was crossing America in 1889 and disliking much of what he saw. Charles E. Rumelin, Portland newspaperman, took Kipling salmon fishing on the Clackamas River. He loved the trip "dripping with sweat, spangled like harlequin with scales, wet from the waist down, nose-peeled by the sun, but utterly, supremely, and consummately happy." "I have lived," he wrote. "The American continent may now sink under the sea, for I have taken the best that it yields, and the best was neither dollars, love, nor real estate."

Dallas (Polk County) June 1, 1907: Elliott family on a Saturday outing in their wagonette built in Dallas. Polk County Courthouse in background. James Elliott is the driver; others are Mrs. Conrad (Millie) Stafrin, Ruby Stafrin Irwin, Mrs. Sam (Florence) Kennedy and her son, Alex Kennedy.

Church services in a 1924 Marmon automobile at Dallas. Driver is Abe Hildbbrand. (Left to right) Frank Holman, Lucretia Holman, Susie Penner, Margaret Penner, Iva Vineyard, Fernando Hockett, the Reverend Clem Swensen, Bert Penner, John Friesen, John F. Buller, Peter D. Ediger.

Dallas (Polk County) about 1910: Man on extreme right is Roe Burnett; other men were probably guests of the hotel. Southern Pacific train No. 76 is ready to leave town for Portland (Engine 1355 Baldwin 4-4-0 built in 1883).

Pacific University Forest Grove 1902: The Archery Club. Women members: Alice Ward, Loli D. McCobb, Caroline McCobb, Mildred Tibbals, Winifred Marsh, Mrs. J. H. Craig, Mrs. Albert R. Sweetser, and Mrs. M. D. Dunning. Man in center: Dr. Henry Liberty Bates. Mascot (small boy): George N. Phinney. Men members: F. S. Barnes, Prof. H. L. Bates, Prof. J. H. Craig, Prof. R. L. V. Lyman, John P. Wagner. Hall in background is Herrick Hall, a girls' dormitory originally called Ladies Hall (1881–1906).

Butteville School in 1925: Two teachers in back row are Harold Aspinwall and Violet Olson. Some of the students are (first row) Elden Pugh, Dorothy Dental, Leroy Pierson, Harold Murray; (second row) Vida White; (third row) Francis Marhoit, Jack Murray, "Bud" Yergen, Willis Mathieu; (fourth row) Philip Yergen, Ralph Pierson, A. D. ("Scotty") Graham, Theora Thamer; (back row) Lucille Raceffe, Jane Yergen, Russel Tauffest.

Forest Grove 1924: Looking north on Main Street at Pacific Avenue just after a fresh Oregon rain. Building in left corner is First National Bank. Automobiles shown are: (right side) 1923 Model T Ford sedan; (left side) 1923 Chevrolet roadster, 1922 Ford Model T touring; 1924 Ford Model T; 1922 Overland; 1924 Ford Model T touring.

Butteville (Marion County): This town, with a history dating back to Pacific Northwest territorial days, today is almost a ghost town. It is located at the edge of French Prairie, sixteen miles up the river from Oregon City. Much of its early-day trade was drawn from prairie ranchers, who were retired French-Canadian trappers of the Hudson's Bay Company. The coming of the river steamers spelled prosperity for the little city. By the end of the Civil War its warehouses were filled with grain and farm products from the surrounding areas. It was an important stop for all steamboats running up and down the Willamette River. The coming of the *Oregon & California Railroad* in 1870 started the decline of Butteville, as much of the traffic formerly carried by water now began moving via rail. (Above) 1910: Butte Avenue looking west, with the Willamette River at the end of the street. Stores on left side of the street belonged to W. R. Scheurer, general merchandise and J. S. Vandeleur & Bentz; grain elevator located at far end of street. Buildings on right side of street: At far end, bordering on river, warehouse originally used by the Hudson's Bay Company as trading post; Episcopal Church, which later became Grange Hall, with a portion of the building leased to the Masonic Lodge; the I.O.O.F. Hall (large building with hitching post in front); and the general merchandise store operated by brothers Josie and William Ryan.

Albany 1909: First Street looking north. The old streetcar, previously pulled by two white horses, was now electrified. All types of transportation can be seen in use. (Extreme left) 1908 one-cylinder Reo owned by Dr. J. L. Hill. (Center) 1906 Rambler touring car owned by James Austin Howard. The Rambler had been brought to Albany on the Willamette River steamboat *Grahamona*. In fact, there were only four automobiles in town; the other two, not shown, were an Oldsmobile belonging to Percy Young and a vehicle owned by Dr. W. H. Davis. All fire engines were pulled by horses. Any horse-drawn dray responding first, after the fire bell rang, would hitch onto the fire engine and gallop to the fire. The owner of the dray received $5.00 for each trip, no matter whether the distance was a block or a mile.

Albany 1923 (Linn County): First Street looking south. Angle parking and many automobiles.

Albany 1909: Six 1909 Rambler automobiles have arrived in one boxcar from Kenosha, Wisconsin. The parade is en route to Howard Rambler garage. Those in first car are (backseat) Fred Munkers, Albany chief of police; W. C. Teabult, first purchaser of one of the new Ramblers; (front seat and driving) James Austin Howard, head of the Howard agency; and (standing on the ground) his son, James Francyl Howard. (Francyl Howard has been editor and publisher of *Albany Greater Oregon* and Corvallis Benton County Herald for many years.)

Albany 1905: L. E. Blain Clothing Company: (Extreme right) Leighton E. Blain, founder. (Left to right) Jay Blain, brother; Archie Hammer, partner; P. A. Goodwin; E. E. Langdon or W. L. Vance. Left front window: men's suits for $12.50 to $15.00 and shoes for $3.00. Right front window: Men's straw or "sailor" hats for 75¢ to $2.00 each. Upstairs window reads Percy R. Kelly, lawyer. This man later became an Oregon Supreme Court justice.

The Aurora Colony was a communal group of old country Germans that came to Oregon during the middle of the nineteenth century. "No man owns anything individually but every man owns everything as a full partner." They followed this type of living for some 25 years during the lifetime of its leaders. These people had an inherent love of music and indulged in it at every opportunity. Throughout the existence of the Colony, and for many years thereafter, Aurora was noted for its fine bands and musicians. In this group are (left to right) A. H. Giesy, cello; Emanuel Keil, first violin; Fred Giesy, clarinet; Henry Giesy, the small boy; William Giesy, second violin; Fred Will, Sr., cornet.

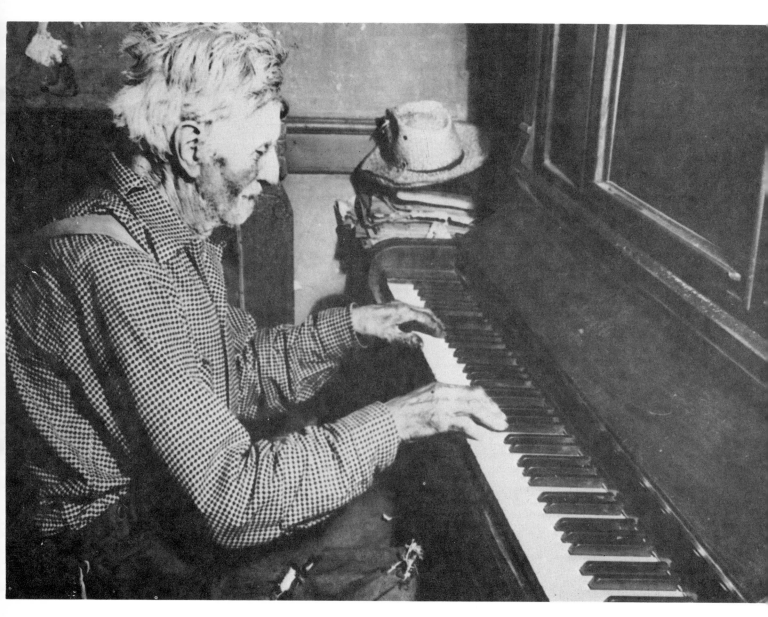

Elias Keil, 81, grandson of the Colony's founder, Dr. William Keil, lived in the weathered mansion built by his grandfather. He was an accomplished pianist and is shown here playing his interpretation of a Strauss waltz. (Right) *Elias Keil's* home as it looked before being restored. Both pictures were taken during the 1940s.

Warren Peter Lee, mail carrier, ready to leave the post office at Canby in 1912.

(Below) Chautauqua headquarters. (Left to right) William H. Dedman, Eva Emery Dye, Mrs. and Mr. Harvey E. Cross, Charles H. Dye, last three unknown. Both pictures were taken at the turn of the century. (Mrs. Eva Emery Dye was a prolific writer of Oregon material, from her first book in 1900 to the publication of her last in 1934. Her writing consisted of poetry, songs, and history, but mostly historical novels.)

Chautauqua Park — Gladstone (Clackamas County) 1910: "Chautauqua Park invites you again to its beautiful park, where a well-filled program will be the delight of all who are seeking rest, recreation, and ennobling influence." (Above) Football game between two of Oregon City's grammar schools (Eastham and Barclay). The Chautauqua auditorium seating 3,000 people, can be seen in background. Streetcars are ready to take football spectators back to Oregon City after the game.

Hubbard 1912: Town band taken in front of Hubbard Hotel, Third and C streets. (Left to right) Andy Beer, alto; Clark Moor Will, first clarient; Ora M. Pulley, alto; unknown; Charles Blosser, alto; Claude Brown, alto; Earl Palmer, clarinet; Ursule B. Wolfer, snare drum; Elton McLaughlin, second clarient (white cap, not in uniform); Frank Fry, bass drum; Clarence Bevens, tuba; Charles M. Will, first cornet; W. R. Hurst, baritone sax; Charles W. Kent, solo cornet; A. D. Wolfer, tenor sax; Dr. A. F. de Lespinasse, band director; George W. Knight, tenor sax. (Old Hubbard Hotel built in 1878 by T. E. James.)

Hubbard 1908 (Marion County): Hubbard folks ready for a Sunday outing, with the men in one car and the women in the other. Photo taken in front of William Miller's pool hall; his living quarters can be seen above. Those in rear car, a 1910 White "gas" car, are (left to right) unknown, Nellie Myrtle Dimick Fry, Lena Miller, Edna Curtis Trillinger. Those in lead car, a 1912 Overland, are Frank Fry (standing), unknown, William Miller, Charles Trillinger, "Si" Yoder, driving.

Gresham (Multnomah County) Gresham Grade School 1896: Back row: H. R. Winchell, principal and upper class teacher; Mrs. Clara Anderson, primary teacher; Miss Hattie Pierce, intermediate grades. Second row: first girl, Maude Cleveland; second girl, Pearl Luella (Ross) Becker. Students shown: Blanche Hannah (Ross) Narver, Joseph Clinton Ross, Lillian Belle Ross, Jane Ellen Ross, Agnes Winchell, Ralph Winchell. Remainder of students shown (last names only): Shattuck, Sleret, Cathey, McCall, Heiney, Lindsay, Miller, Johnson, Smith, Metzger, Roberts, Ruegg, Powell, Duraell. In 1907 above school building was the Gresham Grange Hall. The building was moved east one block from original location on Powell Valley Road.

Gresham 1885: Looking west down Powell Valley Road from Main. On right, Samuel Metzger's 5 and 10 cent store. Next to it, original Gresham Hotel. First building on left, Ford Metzger's saloon. Deep in background, Old White School and Pioneer Baptist Church. Early pioneers shown here are Ben Rollins, Dan Metzger, Jake Metzger, Charles Powell, Ed Sleret, William Knox, George Kinney, John Oregiler, Joe Bouey, Fred Exley, Bob Mason, and Ed Shattuck.

Monmouth Oregon State Normal School (today's Oregon College of Education): Class of 1888 taken in front of Campbell Hall. President D. T. Stanley is on extreme left. Others in the class are Millie Doughty, J. Monroe Powell, Prince L. Campbell, Lena G. Butler, Robert T. Burnett, William S. Carpenter, Sylvester Goodnight, Isabell Gray, Lottie S. Ground, Inez Hamilton, John A. Houck, Lizzie Jakes, C. G. Jones, H. J. Littlefield, Jean McDaniel, E. C. Pentland, Solon Shedd, Ida M. Smith, Thomas A. Wann, Sarah Wimberly, L. May Woodbury, Vida E. Worth, and William L. Worth.

(Above) *McMinnville,* (Yamhill County) taken about 1912: Garage owned by Albert A. Dixon, shown in picture. Identifiable cars are (left to right) 1911 Model AB Maxwell; 1910 Model 10 Buick; 1910 Reo; 1910 Model T Ford; 1910 Model T Ford.

McMinnville: A typical Oregon home in the 1920s. Barn in the background, pump to the right corner, and new Model T Fords.

Mt. Angel (Marion County): A beautiful little city made up of German-Catholic people. 1910 post office with the railroad station in the background. Those shown (left to right) are Arthur Holmes, Henry Aloysius Zollner, Postmaster Thomas L. Ambler, Charles Scharback, unknown.

April 1911 Horse Show.

St. Helens (Columbia County): (Above) 1915 Main Street, with courthouse at the end of the block. Automobiles (right-hand corner) 1913 Model T Ford and 1911 Pierce.

1913 White jitney bus running from Portland to St. Helens and waypoints, owned by Frank Shepard.

Mr. Blous, owner of the Blous Feed Company in Park Place (Clackamas County) personally handles and makes all deliveries in his 1915 Model T Ford.

Lake Oswego: George W. Prosser, his wife, and their two children, Sylver E. and Dana C. en route to church on Sunday morning. Prosser, an early settler in Oswego, was postmaster about 1870 for many years. Much of his property was connected with Oswego Iron Works.

Oswego Iron Works, located 2½ miles west of Oswego: This was the first iron-producing plant to be constructed west of the Rocky Mountains. The first ingots were turned out in 1867. The opening of the first transcontinental railroad into Portland in 1883 was the beginning of the end for this "Pittsburgh of the West." Despite the long distance from iron-producing centers in the eastern states, it was cheaper to make iron there and haul the finished and semi-finished products to the West by rail because of the low grade of ore available here. Today all of the Iron Empire has been converted into costly residential areas, with the exception of the old furnace preserved in the city park (right). Shown in the 1916 picture are Martha Jane (Nicely) Long; her daughter, Ivy Elizabeth Culp, and grandson, Edwin Dawson Culp.

Oswego now called Lake Oswego (Clackamas County): A 1907 view of the city of Oswego, today one of the fastest growing areas in the Pacific Northwest. (Left) State Street, unpaved and with only a few stores. (Center) Southern Pacific station, with a main-line train en route to Corvallis. (Right) The railroad maintained hourly commute service between Portland and Oswego. One of the commute trains can be seen getting "into clear" for the main-line train.

A 1920 view of beautiful Lake Oswego. Swimming in the summertime, much like today, is definitely the word of the day.

Wilsonville 1911: (Above) Dr. William Kettle "IN" his office S.W. Boones Ferry Road. (Below) Dr. William Kettle "OUT" at Roanoke Inn (with the boys). (Left to right) first two men unknown, Joe Chalupsky, William S. Flynn, Jerome Epperly, Dr. William ("Bill") Kettle. Today both these buildings have been dismantled and are now residential areas.

Wilsonville (Clackamas County): The population of this small town in 1910 was 150 people. Today it has shown a sizeable increase and is considered to be one of the fastest growing areas in the Willamette Valley. In 1847 Jesse V. Boone, the great-grandson of Daniel Boone, built a ferryboat on the Willamette River about a mile south of the present Wilsonville site. He cut a road from his ferry, past what is now Wilsonville, through Tualatin into Portland. It became the shortest route from Portland to California. (Above) A 1911 view of the main street showing Doyle General Merchandise, with P. M. Doyle standing in front of his store; Peters and Aden, general merchants, with Jake Peters and D. H. Aden shown. Beyond is a drugstore run by L. F. Darby. The Cottage Hotel is operated by Mrs. E. W. Dill. (Below) A 1911 scene taken in front of the *Oregon Electric Railway* station while the train makes a short stop.

Hillsboro 1909 (Washington County): The post office. (Left to right) lady standing near front door is Bertha Hesse; postman in uniform is Ed Cornelius; man in shirt sleeves is Ben P. Cornelius, postmaster; man on extreme right is Fred Olsen.

An automobile gathering on Main Street, Lebanon, Oregon.

Sodaville 1899 (Linn County near Lebanon) Mineral Springs College: This was a small Presbyterian College founded in 1892, with a curriculum that included literary, scientific, classical, normal, business, theological, and musical courses. The campus consisted of two buildings, the college building on the left and the Ladies Hall on the right. College catalogue read, "Enrollment for 1895 was 125 students. Rent is $2 to $4 per month for a cottage. Students can board themselves at from one dollar to one dollar and fifty cents per week." Somewhat different today! Faculty members and students playing croquet are: (Left to right) first man unknown; Ida S. Geddas, Mrs. H. H. Fuller, Herschel Leroy Mack, Ethel Maria (Starr) Mack. Last five are students, unknown. This college closed in 1904.

Sodaville 1899 (Linn County near Lebanon) Mineral Springs College: The new principal of the normal school, Dr. Herschel Leroy Mack, and his bride, Ethel Maria Starr, have their picture taken in front of their new home. He will teach mathematics, and she will teach literature and art.

The editorial staff of the University of Oregon publication pose for their picture in Eugene about 1910 to prove to the outside world that true Oregonians love the rain. We did not poll each member, but they do look happy. (Left to right) Isabel Jakway, George Goodall, Grace Plummer, Charles Campbell, Amy Holmes, Allen Eaton, J. A. Gamber.

Eugene 1914 (Lane County): At that period the life of a town was usually built around the railroad station. It was from here relatives, friends, and dear ones arrived and departed from the city. As they say, things happened here! (Below) *Southern Pacific* Train No. 19, westbound, heading for San Francisco. The beautiful station grounds with gardens have now been converted to the all-necessary parking areas. Street lighting fixtures, water tower for the engines, mail car next to the locomotive — all gone but not forgotten. SP-2205 (4-6-0) locomotive built in 1888 in Sacramento. Boxlike structure on tender indicates this engine was once a wood burner but has now been converted to oil use.

Eugene — home of the University of Oregon: In 1876 the university had only one building, Deady Hall, which cost the people of Eugene and Lane County some $50,000 to build. There were 5 professors and 177 students on opening day 1876. The building was named after Judge Matthew Paul Deady.

(Below) *Eugene* 1923 (Lane County): Looking west on Willamette Street.

The history of steamboating in Oregon waters, from the beginning, has abounded in thrilling interest. The *Lot Whitcomb* was the first river steamer built in Oregon, followed by the *Jennie Clark,* the first stern-wheeler. When the *Jennie Clark* took to the waters in 1855, her speed and movability surpassed the larger *Lot Whitcomb.* Sternwheelers became very popular in Oregon and for the next thirty years were the lifeblood of our state transportation system. (Above) *Clatskanie* about 1915 (Columbia County): *Beaver* ran between Clatskanie and Portland for many years, assisting Simon Benson Logging Company and handling forest products.

Newburg (Yamhill County): *Southern Pacific's* first Red Electric arrived Saturday, January 17, 1914, with six new steel cars. In order to get the train through the center of town, "old two spot," as the Charles K. Spaulding Logging Company's switch engine was called, was pressed into service to haul these cars from the main line through town and back to the main line again. This short section of the line had no overhead wiring as yet. Old No. 2 had Engineer T. Gardner and Fireman John Lueders, who backed their engine down and coupled onto the special electric train and with many a snort and puff pulled it into town.

Elliott Ford Agency on Main Street near Fourth in Oregon City handling the 1912 and 1915 Model T Fords. Inside the garage can be seen the owners, Mr. and Mrs. Chester A. Elliott.

Oregon City 1915: *Grahamona,* a stern-wheeler of the *Yellow Stack* built in 1912, passes through the lock at Oregon City en route up the Willamette River to Champoeg and Salem. The lock, built in 1873, is still in use.

Oregon City 1912 — Pacific Highway Garage at Twelfth and Main streets: Mort E. Park, owner, with his sister, Maude Park. Automobiles (left to right) 1911 Model T Ford; next three cars are 1911 EMFs.

Oregon City about 1890: The boardwalk to Canemah at the end of Main Street on a Sunday afternoon, when some of the young folk gather for a little socializing.

Oregon City 1905: Company of Oregon City girls organized and drilled by James P. Shaw to take part in the exercises of the Grand Army Encampment held in Oregon City in 1905. These girls are marching on Main Street, and streetcar tracks can be seen.

Oregon City 1894 — Main Street looking north: The *East Side Railway Company* was a new electrified, long-distance car line of some thirteen miles between Portland and Oregon City and was the first trolley line of its kind in the entire nation. Each trolley car was given a girl's name (note *Kate* and *Dora*). This presented some interesting problems in giving orders such as Nora's "underskirt" needs repair or Dora's "clapper" is loose. Each trolley car was eventually given a number. (Center) Electric Hotel, so named because the word "electricity" was very important and revered at that date. On the ground floor was Leonard Charman and George Eastham's drugstore.

Oregon City 1899 — Frank Busch general store: Bird cages — cook stoves — copper boilers — tea kettles. You name it and we'll have it! Employees shown (left to right): Frank Whitman, Roscoe Frost, Frank Busch (man with hat), John Busch, Rose Muller, Nora Hanifan. Woman and children in background unknown.

Oregon City 1910: Interior view of barber shop run by Edward L. Johnson, at rear. Other barbers shown are George Campbell, William C. Green, and Fred A. Miller.

Many types and designs of early bicycles were invented, but the most acceptable was the highwheeler. It had almost a fanatical following among the young handlebar-mustache crowd. There was a challenge about riding these machines (proper balance, pedalling, steering, and holding one's poise) that offered appeal much as we find among hot rodders today. Bicycles were becoming so popular that safety improvements were offered on the new models. Strange as it seems, the young handlebar crowd retorted with "Designing a safe bicycle is like hobbling a spirited horse." Making bicycles "more respectable" for a woman was a problem; exposing her ankle while riding was a serious misdemeanor. Bicycling for women really came into its own when ladies' bloomers were considered acceptable dress; previous to this, they were worn by eccentrics and "dare me" types. As bloomers became acceptable, bicycles became as popular with women as they were with men. (Above) Corvallis July 4, 1888 (Benton County): Seven young men in front of the S. B. Grayam photo shop. (Left to right) Jean Titus, Carl St. Luedermen, Irvine N. Smith, Percy A. Young, Notman S. Smith, Jone St. Rude, J. Price Hail. (Below) Near *Philomath* 1910 (Benton County): *Oregon Agricultural College* students (now Oregon State University) bicycling on an average road after a rainy period.

Oregon Agricultural College girls (now Oregon State University) out for a bicycle ride about 1900.

Oregon State University (at one time called Oregon Agriculture College): First women's class in horticulture. (Left to right) Martha Avery, granddaughter of the founder of Corvallis; Leona Louis; Rose Horton; Anna Allen; Anna Denman; Minnie Waggoner; Ida Ray; and Professor George Coote. College Administration Building in background.

The Lebanon (Linn County) Volunteer Fire Department competing in the state fire-fighting contest held in Corvallis in 1916. The team consisted of (left to right) Gordon Griffith, D. A. Reeves, Lloyd Tucker, Glen Tucker, M. J. Gilson, Vern Reeves, Arthur Scott, L. Stacey, and Carl Blatchley.

Corvallis & Alsea River Railroad, showing all its motive power in 1910. Trackage consisted of twenty-six miles from Corvallis to Glenbrook and Monroe. Directors of the line were F. L. Miller; B. W. Johnson; A. W. Fischer; and J. Ed Williams. C&AR No. 1 is a 4-6-0 Baldwin; C&AR No. 2 is a Heisler locomotive.

Corvallis 1923 — Second and Madison streets looking west: City Hall can be seen in center-left with conning-roof tower. Automobiles are (left to right) 1922 Chevrolet 490 Model sedan, 1923 Model T Ford delivery van, Lincoln bus, 1919 Winton (directly behind the policeman), 1919 seven-passenger Studebaker (facing policeman), 1922 Model T Ford (first car on extreme right).

Brownsville 1910 (Linn County): Rufus Winfield Tripp (standing on the ground), realtor from Albany, with two carloads of clients looking for farms in the surrounding area. Homeseekers saw the great potential of living in the Oregon country. In the background is the John Moyer home, Italian-villa style, built in 1881 and today being restored to its original condition by the Linn County Historical Society. The two automobiles shown are a 1909 Ford (front) and a 1910 Reo.

(Above) Taken in the Willamette Valley around 1900: A Standard Oil man sells kerosene, a fuel necessary to keep the lamps in the home burning before the coming of electric lights. Horses have a twinelike string material over their bodies; the movement of these cords protects them against insects.

Cottage Grove 1903 (Lane County): The city's first hospital, built and operated by Drs. Henry C. and Katherine Schleef and located on the north side of Main Street. (Left) Dr. Henry C. holds a baby while Dr. Katherine looks on. (Center) Directly under the City Hospital ws the furniture and undertaking business operated by Monroe Biven and Schuyler Lauder. (Right) The hardware store run by Harry F. Wynne.

Dundee (Yamhill County): Dundee Public School 1909. Grades one through four were taught *downstairs* by Stella Warner (left in back row). Grades five through eight were taught *upstairs* by Principal Amos Stanbrough (extreme right in picture).

Wilhoit Mineral Springs 1903 (Clackamas County) near Scotts Mills: A few years ago this was a well-known health and pleasure resort. Men in back are George Scholl, George Will, and Antone Will. The women in the center are Elizabeth Forstern, Anna Will, Elizabeth Will, Triphina Forstner Will, Myra Will, and Augusta Snyder Will.

Horse-drawn street cleaner at work in Silverton in 1911. It was a fortunate city that could afford one of these newly invented machines.

Springwater post office in 1910: "Small town of 300 people located on Clear Creek, settled in 1852, 27 miles southeast from Portland and near Estacada. W. J. Lewellen was postmaster and ran the general merchandise store. Bitner, Boylan & Company, spool mill, was the town's only industry." Description further stated, "They had two mail deliveries daily and one RFD route."

Liberal about 1913 (Clackamas County): W. J. E. Vick merchandise store with Mr. Vick standing in front door. Automobile is believed to be a 1911 Kissel. In buggy to left is Charles Fisher; driver in auto is Grover Fredericks; in backseat is Barney Fredericks; in second buggy are Mr. and Mrs. Casper Zinger; with cart is Charles H. Calahan.

Mill City (Marion County) taken about 1895 showing the arrival of the *Oregon Pacific Railroad Company* mixed train* pulled by No. 7, a woodburning 4-4-0 Cooke locomotive.

_____

*A mixed train is one that handles both freight and passenger cars.

Deer Island 1911 (Columbia County): While speeding along the Columbia River Highway today one might be a little puzzled to see a town called Deer Island, as this is not an island nor can one be seen. There is an island not too far away in the Columbia River, and from this the small town was named. We were told the men on the horses are M. W. Brown, justice of the peace, and Charles Smith, manager of the local hotel. (Right) Schoolteacher and children unknown.

Estacada 1910 (Clackamas County): "Hotel Estacada, a modest, homelike, and comfortable inn, where the visitor may make his home and headquarters during his vacation." So read the advertising material published by Oregon Water Power & Railway Company to encourage traffic over its interurban line. It offered a real bargain for those seeking a delightful and enjoyable weekend vacation; but, alas, Henry's Model T brought this type of close-in entertainment to an end. The woodburning steam engine, OWP-112, is a 4-4-0 Baldwin built in 1882.

Jessie Maggie Heath and Ivy Blanche Heath Hall, two ladies with sailor hats, en route to church on Sunday morning. They would use the railroad speeder for an eleven-mile downhill "ride and pump" to Gates. After they attended church and had a short visit with friends, the daily *Corvallis & Eastern* passenger train would carry them back to Hall's Station, a small logging camp owned by Spruce Vale Hall. They would ride in the passenger coach and the speeder in the baggage car.

Barton 1911 (Clackamas County): Residents of this town include H. F. Gibson, general merchandise; J. D. Morris, postmaster; A. E. Alspaugh; and C. A. Burkhardt.

Falls City July 4, 1905 (Polk County): Falls City has several good-sized lumber mills. In 1903 the Gerlinger people built the *Salem Falls City & Western Railway* from Dallas to Falls City, resulting in further development of Falls City. Dwellings shown on top of hill (left to right): first house unknown, middle house belonged to J. R. Moyer, Professor H. C. Seymor of the Falls City grade school (shown at end) boarded here. The house on the extreme right, down the hill, belonged to Mr. Toller, the baker. The loggers are celebrating the Fourth of July with the annual contest of "bucking logs" or falling timber. Material was furnished by Bryan-Lucas Lumber Company and Falls City Lumber Company owned by Grahame Griswold. Man in center is one of the judges.

Hoskins (Benton County): The roundhouse grounds of the *Valley & Siletz Railroad,* taken in 1938. V&S-50 (2-6-2 Baldwin) woodburning locomotive has been equipped with a Gerlinger spark arrester on the stack to prevent forest fires. To the right can be seen V&S-5, gasoline motor built by Hofius Steel & Equipment Company, Seattle.

Yamhill stage ready to leave on its forty-five-mile trip to Tillamook, shown in front of the F. L. Trullinger post office and store. The stage left Yamhill at 4 A.M. and reached Tillamook that same evening if the roads and weather were satisfactory. The stage fare was $5.00 one-way; the driver is believed to be Jim Messinger. The small town of Yamhill is a farming community and prides itself that the movie actress, Mary Pickford, once lived here.

Springfield 1905 (Lane County): 1904 one-cylinder Cadillac stops in front of Springfield Hotel. Campaign poster in hotel window supports Gov. George Earle Chamberlain.

Walterville about 1905 (Lane County): A new homesteader arrives in Oregon with all his worldly possessions on one wagon. His first acquaintance is the J. W. Shumate General Merchandise Store. In the extreme background is J. W. Shumate. On the wagon is Cash Mead, and the little girl is Kate, J. W. Shumate's daughter.

Willamette Falls Railway in West Linn as it looked in 1910. At that time the line was owned by *Portland Railway Light & Power Company*. The white trolley car served the passenger operation, while the electric locomotive is pulling an empty log flatcar used for moving cottonwood to the paper mill. *Willamette Falls Railway* station, in background, is on the same location as the library today.

Shedd 1903 (Linn County): The last day of school. The town is on hand to honor Mr. and Mrs. Grimes (directly behind the sign), for their years of teaching. People just behind the Grimes are Riley C. Margason, Charles Arnold, Mary E. Duncan, Emmett E. Coon, Katie Baton, Sophia Thompson, Emma Arnold. Some of the people on left end: M. G. Coon, R. A. Jayne, J. C. Shedd, A. Sutherland, A. B. Wilmot, J. H. Austin.

Two covered bridges side-by-side across Thomas Creek in Linn County near Scio. One is Gilkey Bridge and the other is Southern Pacific. Water barrels on top of railroad bridge are to be used in case of fire.

1st Street, Independence, Oregon.

Schnoerr Park, located in the small town of Willamette near Oregon City, in 1912 offered a gathering place for various groups on Sunday afternoon. Here is a group of German extraction. Dr. Nash, a dentist, sits in his 1914 White automobile; Frank Busch is man standing in front row; Gustav Schnoerr is man in front row without a coat; and Mr. and Mrs. Ernest Mass are at extreme right end.

Near *Dayton* (Yamhill County): Capt. Medorem Crawford (1819-1891) was one of the grand old pioneers of early Oregon. His account of his journey over the Oregon Trail in 1842 under the leadership of Dr. Elijah White offers fascinating reading. The *Oregonian* commented on his life: "He was known to every person in Oregon during many years and remembered by all who retained recollections of early days in Oregon. Medorem Crawford was a man to fix the impress of his individuality and character upon any community. As a pioneer he was among the most intelligent, far-seeing, and energetic; as a state-builder, he bore a very important part." He was present at the Wolf Meetings at Champoeg when Oregon took the first steps in forming a government for the vast Oregon Country. He ran a portage service with ox and cart around the falls at Oregon City. He was an army captain and a provisional Oregon government legislator. Photo made about 1890 as he was spending his last days with his son. (Left to right) Medorem Crawford; Leroy Crawford, his brother; Mary Crawford Stevens, his daughter; John Morrison Crawford, his son; Mrs. John Crawford, his daughter-in-law.

(Left) The people of Scio (Linn County) were very disappointed when the narrow-gauge railroad being constructed down the valley missed their small community by two miles. These ambitious people constructed two miles of trackage from Scio to make a connection with the Southern Pacific at a point known as West Scio. Members of the town took turns working and keeping up the right-of-way and trackage. Photo shows some of Scio's leading people in front of their only handcar, itself a symbol of accomplishment. Small boy is Albert Deforest Woodmansee, whose mother, Mary Elizabeth Woodmansee, was the local agent for the Southern Pacific at the West Scio railroad station. Some of the others interested in keeping the two-mile line running were Albert Woodmansee Sr., Fred Daly, Andrew Hagey, Cobe Cyrus, John M. V. Bilyeu, Sterling P. Munkers, Edward Goin. Photo taken about 1900.

(Left) *Cornelius* 1911 (Washington County): Hotel Oregon
managed by Mrs. Emaline Hughes.

Near *Creswell:* This bridge, built across the Coast Fork of the
Willamette River about 1874, no longer exists. Those in pic-
ture are John Whiteaker, Oregon's first governor; L. N.
Roney, builder of the bridge; Riley Petty and his dog; George
Petty, his father; Cris Weintzenreid.

See the countryside on a Sunday afternoon by riding the interurban cars. Scene at Boring railroad station, a small town
in Clackamas County a short distance from Portland.

(Above) *Clackamas* 1915 (near Oregon City): Train arriving with wives and sweethearts on a Sunday visit to the Oregon National Guard encampment. Automobiles shown are (front to back) 1910 White, 1913 Overland, 1914 Model T Ford, 1915 Model T Ford.

(Below) *Chemawa Indian School* (1910) Marion County near Salem: U.S. government offered full education privileges to the American Indian.

Portland Railway Light & Power Company private car *Portland,* running special for a ladies' group, taken about 1911 at River Mill near Estacada.

Whiteson 1885 (Yamhill County near McMinnville): Town originally called *White's* named after Henry White, early farmer. This small settlement was the crossing place of two railroads, *Oregonian Railway Company, Limited,* a narrow-gauge line, and The *Western Oregon Railroad,* standard-gauge line. The railroads were rivals and made no effort to offer connections from one line to another, forcing people to stay all night in hotel seen in background. Engine No. 5 was a small Porter-built locomotive with a 2-6-0 classification. Wood is for powering the locomotive. This train ran from Portland to Airlie in Polk County, passing through Oswego, Newburg, Dallas, and Monmouth. Those shown are (left to right) Charles Young, brakeman; W. Ellis, fireman; Charles Mahony, engineer; and Lou Keyser, brakeman (sitting on pilot). John M. Poorman, conductor, is not shown.

North Santiam 1905 (Marion County): A typical rural scene in the *Willamette Valley*. (Left to right) The Millie Bunnell home, formerly North Santiam (subscription) grade school; Protestant Community Church; Southern Pacific *North Santiam* railroad station (open air and only offering protection from the rain); Artilla Jane Chance home and farm buildings. Note dirt road, two standing fir trees, and a few slabwood sticks (right). The wood was shipped out by the carload to points in the valley to be used for home heating and cooking. This was before oil and gas furnaces came into use.

French Prairie area in the Willamette Valley near Woodburn. George Graves in his new 1904 imported French Renault automobile. Always good to have a friend on hand in case one needs a tire pumped up. Note wicker box attached to the car. Does it contain a lunch, or is it full of tools to repair the car?

Willamette Valley & Cascade Mountains Military Wagon Road Company was in 1861 a toll road. Entrance is shown here. Sign gives charges for using the road.

TOLL RATES ON THE W.V.&C.M. WAGON ROAD
TO THE DESCHUTES RIVER

For 6 Horse Teams	$3.50	For Pack Animals	.50¢
" 4 " "	3.00	" Loose Horse & Per Head	.20¢
" 2 " "	2.00	" " Cattle " "	.10¢
" 1 " "	1.00	" " Sheep " "	.03¢
" Horse & Rider	.75¢	" " Hogs " "	.03¢

TO UPPER SODA SPRINGS & FISH LAKE ROUND TRIP

For 4 Horse Teams	$1.50	For Horse & Rider	.25¢
" 2 " "	1.00	" Pack Animals	.50¢
" 1 " "	.50¢		

NOTICE. TO ANY PERSON OR PERSONS TRAVELING OVER THIS ROAD NEGLECTING OR REFUSING TO PAY TOLL WILL BE LIABLE TO BE PROSECUTED & BE MADE TO PAY THREE TIMES THE AMOUNT OF THE TOLL.

John Frederick Becker, Columbia County farmer, displays his new Maxwell automobile costing $675. His older brother, Nicholas Becker is behind.

Emmett Walton Williams, a brakeman on the *Corvallis & Eastern* Railroad. He just turned twenty years of age and has a new uniform and a new job. Williams served as a Southern Pacific train conductor for many years.

EASTERN OREGON

Arrival of the U.S. mail in Burns about 1915. Mamie Winters, postmaster, is beside mail; other party unknown. Upstairs is office of Charles A. Byrd of *Harney County News*.

Long Creek 1890 (Grant County): I.O.O.F. (Oddfellows) band marches on Main Street of Long Creek. Some of the buildings and people are Oril L. Patterson, editor of *Long Creek Eagle;* E. O. Woodall, the postmaster; C. E. Dustin, C. W. Conger, J. A. Larribee, E. A. Knight, T. B. Hall, John Blackwell, D. W. Shaw, J. M. Connaway, William Lewis, Oscar Reinhart, D. A. Meincke.

Dixie 1909 (Grant County): One of the stops on the daily Sumpter Valley Railroad narrow-gauge line running from Baker to Prairie City. The automobile is believed to be a 1909 Pierce. Directly behind it is the railroad station. The stages make a connection with the train.

An eastern Oregon farmhouse of the 1900s. Occupants proudly display new 1903 Olds, resulting in less use of the Sunday hammock. Note rainbarrel at side of house.

Austin 1890 (Grant County): This was one of the primary stops on the stage route from Prairie City to Baker and was in use long before the Sumpter Valley Railroad Company thought of laying a track through the area. These stages carried passengers and mail.

Prairie City (Grant County): (Above) 1890 Prairie City stage arrives from Canyon City. Driver is either Rollo Johnson or Archie Timms; man without a coat is believed to be William E. Weir, publisher of *Prairie City Miner,* whose office can be seen behind the stage.

Granite (Grant County): Gold was discovered July 4, 1862, and soon there were 5,000 people here, plus another 4,000 Chinese. When the gold was exhausted the town dwindled to some 50 people, and today it's a ghost town. (Left) Granite Hotel built in 1900 by Grant Thornburg, who can be seen standing near front door. The hotel was a three-story structure having some thirty rooms. The important people were on hand as the stage arrived. Some of them are Postmaster L. N. Ford, Loren L. Forrest, L. C. Haynes, James H. Hilliard, B. W. Levens, J. Marott, W. B. Nillenghby, A. V. Oliver, Thomas H. Boynton, W. B. Sargent, E. D. Steincamp, L. W. Stutts.

Canyon City 1895: Moving a heavy boiler to one of the mines in the area. In the background can be seen the *News* office. (Left to right) Charles Guernsey, on horse; O. Guernsey, talking to Bob Glenn. (Extreme right) Sheriff Newt Livingston. Others unknown.

STAGE FROM AUSTIN TO BURNS

The coming of the Concord stagecoach added another important chapter to the history of transportation in this state. The packmule and prairie schooner departed with the coming of this stage. No vehicle has ever been devised by human ingenuity that could negotiate rough or unsurfaced highways like the Concord. Ruts, rocks, and small logs were no obstruction to its movement. Here is one of these coaches running between Austin and Burns in Eastern Oregon.

Sumpter 1900: Sumpter stages ready to depart for interior points in Baker and surrounding counties. The Concord stages served off-rail mines with U.S. mail and express.
Thomas McEwen owned and operated the stage line.

In front of the Sumpter Hotel 1902: A group from the local Community Church are about to enjoy a Sunday school picnic with lots of homemade ice cream and banana cream cake. Note plank paving in street. As Brooks Hawley, an old-time resident, describes it, "That was Sumpter's pride and joy to stay out of the mud and the dust." The W. R. Hawley store is the one with the awnings. At the extreme left can be seen little round windows in the brick of the First National Bank. The Sumpter Hotel was a very commodious one with a fine restaurant and modern accommodations, including steam heat, electric lights, and all. The building was constructed of brick and was believed fireproof. However, the fire of August 13, 1917 destroyed the structure, leaving only a few bricks to mark the site.

The saloon in the Sumpter Hotel: Note the towels for your hands, also the case holding choice cigars. Your worth and standing were measured by the price you paid for your smokes. Note gaslight fixture.

The First National Bank of Sumpter. It would appear these men are well-to-do depositors for the bank.

The town of Sumpter today is almost a ghost town. Little semblance is left of the might and power it expressed during the lucrative mining days. It is said Sumpter was only a small camp before the arrival of the Sumpter Valley Railroad in 1895. By 1904, it is reported, the population reached 3,500. Sumpter will always be remembered as a station on the Sumpter Valley Railroad. This particular rail line has obtained a "mark of excellence" that no other rail carrier in the state can hope to reach. Here is a picture of the Sumpter Valley train operating on the narrow-gauge line between Baker and Prairie City.

(Right) *Sumpter* 1905: Fred Jamison (right), a resident of this town for many years, shows the outside of his "Bachelor's Heaven." Note the Webster's Unabridged Dictionary used while rocking out in the open in his favorite chair, the nearby hammock, and a reliable bicycle for transportation. He had, it seems, all the finer necessities of life.

(Above) *Sumpter* 1900: A boiler for the Red Boy Mine being delivered with fifteen or sixteen pair of horses. The boiler has just arrived by railroad. Wheels on wagon have iron fitted to solid sections of logs. Smokestack to the right is the steam electric power plant, fired up only at night, as this was the only time they needed any electricity. Photo made in front of the Sumpter Valley Railroad Station.

Sumpter, showing the First National Bank in 1902, with President and Mrs. Steincamp inside the bank.

Cornucopia (Baker County): A ghost town today. This town was once a rip-roaring gold mining camp with more than 1,000 people. It boomed not once but several times, as each new lode of fabulously rich ore was discovered. The first big boom years were 1884-86. (Above) Cornucopia as it looked about 1890 to 1900. Girls on hotel balcony are "waving" to some of the miners as they come into town.

Baker 1897: Inside the Basche Hardware Store, founded in 1875 and very much in operation today. (Left to right) Extreme left, first man: Nathaniel Cooper, bookkeeper. (Center with hat): Peter Basche, the founder of the store. (Right, woman): Adele Pefferle, store attendant. Others unknown.

Baker about 1890: Entrance to Samuel Solomon's Clothing House and to Saddle & Harness Shop owned by John B. Griswold and Mrs. T. P. Henderson.

Baker 1898: Looking north on Main Street during the Fourth of July festivities. Note horse-drawn streetcar. When the horse-drawn car was retired it ended the service; the city never electrified the line.

Baker 1880s: Syrenus Burnett McCord's agricultural implements and blacksmith shop.

The Steam Locomotive: (Above) Taken at Baker about 1890 in front of the *Oregon Railway & Navigation Company* railroad station (Union Pacific today). Locomotive shown was ORN-76 (4-6-0) coal-burner built by Manchester in 1883.

(Below) Robert Nelson McCord and Berthold Newberger celebrate the Fourth of July 1905 in their 1904 Oldsmobile. This was Baker's first automobile. Note license plate "ORE 155." Registration was secured from the capital in Salem for 25¢. You could then, if you liked, send to Boise, Idaho, for a metal plate showing your license number.

Pendleton 1913: The first carload of 1913 Ford roadsters unloaded in this city. They were consigned to Oregon Motor Garage and arrived in an end-door boxcar on *Oregon Railway & Navigation Company.* All automobiles shipped by rail were shipped without fenders. These were attached by consignee after unloading. B. F. Trombley is in charge.

Pendleton 1902: Main Street of the city. Hack (right) is driven by Edward Alexander Culp.

Pendleton about 1915: The Westward Ho Parade has become one of the outstanding history-oriented parades in the country. When Round-up officials first started a parade, they put together dray horses, cowboys, Indians, and equipment of various types including automobiles and, for that matter, almost anything they could get hold of. This is one of the annual Round-up parades as it wound its way through the streets of Pendleton. People came from many miles to take in the grandeur of the early days of the West. Automobile in center is 1909 Franklin.

Pendleton 1910 (Umatilla County): A family has its picture taken in front of an Indian tepee on the Umatilla Indian Reservation. The automobile is a 1908 Model 10 Buick. The city of Pendleton extends to the edge of the reservation.

Walter Glen Hanna's *Vale Meat Market* in 1915, showing him behind the counter. His father, George Hanna, and sister, Jennie Townsend, are also shown. (Malheur County).

Frenchglen is hardly more than a wide spot in the road in southeastern Oregon. The town is named after Peter French, who controlled all the land between Winnemucca, Nevada, and Burns, Oregon. A hundred men patrolled his ranch to guard his cattle and discourage would-be homesteaders. Shown is Frenchglen Hotel — formerly a hotel in Blitzen, Oregon, but moved here. Following this can be seen the post office and the general store.

(Above) *Burns* 1915 (Harney County): The Sagebrush Symphony. This orchestra was featured on the Edward Hines Lumber Company float in the Fourth of July parade. Some of the musicians are Mrs. William Farre, Trilby Whitaker Bennett, M. V. Dodge, Frank Loggan, Baxter Reed, Kathleen Jordan, Geary Clevenger, Gwendolyn Lampshire Hayden, Alex Eggleston, Roselle Reed, Francis King Terrell, Ted Reed, Jo Young, Terrance Haney, Margaret Welcome Jetly, Ruby Owsley, and Ruby Campbell Cole. The arranger was Mary Thompson Dodge, and her four-year-old son is the trumpeter in dark knickers.

(Below) Guests at the lodge at Lehman Hot Springs, a popular resort a few miles from Pendleton, are taken on a berry-picking outing and picnic during the summer of 1912. The cook at the resort has prepared a delightful luncheon for all to enjoy. Lady with a big hat in the center of wagon is Ivy Elizabeth Culp, and man driving the mules wearing a sailor hat is her husband, Edward Alexander Culp. Photo was taken by Walter Scott Bowman, a Umatilla photographer well known for his early pictures of the rodeo bucking at the annual Pendleton Round-up.

Umatilla County Indians meet President Warren G. Harding.

Brogan 1905 (Malheur County): A close-up view of the home located in the center of the large Edwards Ranch. (Left to right) hired man unknown, Harry Clay Edwards, Willard R. Edwards, Sarah Francis Edwards, Clarice Barbara Edwards, Irma E. Edwards, John Stephen Edwards, Phil Emit Edwards. In the upstairs window are Alma Edwards and Pearl E. Edwards.

CENTRAL OREGON

Stagecoach leaving on the return trip from Cloud Cap Inn to Hood River. Mount Hood (11,245 feet) can be seen in the background. An 1890 schedule was as follows. From Portland to Hood River via Union Pacific train or steamer *Bailey Gatzert*:

Lv. Hood River	Stagecoach for the next 10 miles
Ar. Little Luckamas	(Luncheon)
Lv. Little Luckamas	Stagecoach with 4 fresh horses
Lv. Elk Beds	Stagecoach with 6 fresh horses
	(straining at their bits pulling the passengers
	up the final miles to Cloud Cap Inn)

The trip from Hood River to Cloud Cap Inn (altitude 5,860 feet) took five and a half hours. Built in 1889, the inn is still in use today.

Rhododendron 1914 (Clackamas County): Rhododendron Inn, built about 1910 by Lee Holden, former Portland fire chief, was located on the Mount Hood Highway forty-six miles from Portland. Automobiles of that time could make the trip in about three hours. The fourteen-room inn was located beside the Zig Zag River, and the surrounding area was made up of stately spruce, fir, and oak trees. The inn burned in 1949. Automobiles shown (left to right): 1912 Regal, 1910 American Underslung, 1912 Model T Ford, and it is believed the last car is a 1908 Rambler.

Mountaineers ready to depart for the climb up Mount Hood. Catwalk on top of the inn is for observation.

In 1908-1909, news that railroad service would soon extend to central Oregon started one of the last great rushes for 750,000 acres of government homestead lands. During this period, photographer Benjamin Arthur Gifford often saw large groups of new settlers coming into the area. Here are some of those wagon trains. Gifford's own wagon is in the picture.

The Needles or *Pillars of Hercules,* often referred to as *Speelyai's Children.* Speelyai is the name of the coyote god of the mid-Columbia region. According to Indian legend, Speelyai's wife and two sons were attempting to escape from him. He became enraged when they refused to return home. He transformed his wife into a waterfall, now called Latourelle, and, with his power of enchantment, willed that his two sons should stand where they were, each a pillar of rock. They are with us today and can be seen as we journey up the Columbia River Highway.

When Henry Villard was building the *Oregon Railway & Navigation Company* up the Columbia River he laid his tracks directly between the *Needles*. He must have had a premonition that the two brothers were quarreling. ORN-84, passing through the Needles headed westbound, is Rhode Island class locomotive 4-4-0 built in 1890. (Above): After the Union Pacific Railroad took over the ORN it relaid the tracks beyond the Needles and closer to the Columbia River. The railroad must have believed that the quarrel was over, so legend has it.

UP-3209, eastbound, is a Baldwin locomotive class 4-6-2 built in 1906.

Memaloose Island — 14 miles west of The Dalles in Wasco County: For countless ages before the white man came, the native Indian tribes deposited their dead on this Island in "dead houses" built above the ground. The Indians knew their dead were safe here from predatory animals. At times high water from the Columbia River would wash many of the bones away. Victor Trevitt, an 1851 pioneer from New England and resident of The Dalles, died in 1883 and requested his remains be interred on the island. "I'll take my chances with the Indians in the Resurrection," he said. After the Indians discovered this, they never again buried their own dead on the island; in fact, many removed their relatives, believing the area had been contaminated by allowing a white man to be buried here.

Multnomah Falls 1917 (Multnomah County): Often called the Queen of Cataracts it has its rise in Larch Mountain, an extinct volcano. Some of the automobiles shown (left to right): 1915 Model T Ford, 1915 Dodge, 1916 Studebaker, unknown (man bending over back tire), 1913 Moline, 1913 Buick roadster in back.

Chanticleer Inn (Multnomah County near Crown Point): This inn, built in 1912, was a famous Columbia River landmark. It was owned and managed by Mrs. Marie Morgan. At first it was necessary to use the railroad and detrain at Rooster Rock, but after the opening of the Columbia River Highway in 1915 it became a delightful Sunday afternoon drive. The food was delicious, and the view was something to remember. The inn burned October 8, 1930. (Above) Photo taken about 1917 show a 1913 Studebaker facing the camera, along with many other cars. The famous Chanticleer Inn can be seen in the background.

Viento is a small lumbering town eight miles west of Hood River and owned by *Oregon Lumber Company*. Stacks of finished lumber can be seen, with the Columbia River in the background. The westbound passenger train of *Oregon Railway & Navigation Company* is stopped, probably unloading passengers and U.S. mail. Water tank beside the tracks is for use of the steam locomotive. David Eccles owns the mill. Some of the other employees are William Eccles, G. H. Carver, J. Hanson, Joel Nibley, R. E. Hill, Dave Steinberg, W. A. Morgan, J. H. Jarvis, James F. Murray, and John Northup.

Bailey Gatzert — another of the pleasure boats on the Oregon River. Photo taken from the bow looking back towards the pilot house. People are drinking in the Oregon beauty under the bright sun.

(Below left) *Heppner* 1918 (Morrow County): The Oregon Railway & Navigation Company noon passenger train arrives. Frank Gilliam and L. E. Bisbee, owners of the local hardware store, send their wagon to the railroad station to meet the train. The automobile shown is a 1914 Model T Ford truck.

Mitchell Point Tunnel 1919 (Hood River County): The Columbia River Highway passed through a 385-foot rock tunnel lighted by five windows. It was constructed by convict labor and opened in 1920. Today it is a sealed tomb, having been blasted away in 1954 to make room for a new four-lane highway. The Alfred L. Stones are riding in a new 1919 Oldsmobile.

Shaniko called itself the wool capitol of the world, possibly a slight exaggeration, but it was a collecting point of all the central Oregon wool producers and farmers. Note (right) the large wool warehouse, with wagon pulled by four pair of horses. In the background (left) can be seen the railroad station for old Columbia Southern that operated a daily train from Shaniko to a connection with the Union Pacific at Biggs, Oregon, a distance of sixty-nine miles.

Shaniko, incorporated in 1901, was a real western town much like we see on TV today, with its saloons, gambling houses, bawdy houses, and all. The town never became quite big enough or bad enough to call in Marshall Wyatt Earp, but it did have a strong western melodramatic flavor. John Wilcox was the first postmaster, back in 1900. Today Alice Vivian Wilcox Roberts still keeps the post office running. Photo taken in 1912.

Lenora Hunter, Postmaster of Mosier (Wasco County) Oregon, September, 1914.

Mayor of Moro, Walter H. Moore, drives his new 1909 Oldsmobile with his wife, Laura Cushman Moore. In backseat is Ernest H. Moore, local businessman and farmer, with Laura Ireland. Sherman County Courthouse, seen in background, was built in 1899 and is still in use today.

John Monroe De Moss and his wife of two weeks have their picture taken at the entrance to their ranch in Sherman County in their new 1916 Overland. To make the picture more complete they waited for the *Columbia Southern Railroad* train to pass.

Madras May 11, 1911 (Jefferson County): Barnes Circus parade, reported to be the first held in this town, marches down the main street. Some of the buildings in the background are the post office (Fred Davis, postmaster); Madras Trading Company (C. E. Roush, owner); harness store (J. E. Wilson, owner); cigar store (Perry Wible, proprietor); and general merchandise store (A. G. Sanford, operator).

Bend about 1910 (Deschutes County): A freight wagon arrives on Wall Street with two trailer wagons and an eight-horse dragline team owned by Harvy Filey, who is riding one of the rear horses. Much of the freight was handled in this manner. In the background can be seen the post office (Alfred H. Grant, postmaster). The building in the middle is the drugstore owned and operated by C. W. Merrill. He also owns the 1909 Overland behind the wagon. This automobile was the first owned by a Bend resident. The last building (extreme right) is H. A. Hill's meat market.

Hood River (Hood River County): "The man who settles in the Hood River valley, 'the University of Apple Culture,' has the assurance of liberal remuneration for his labor and capital. In addition to this, he will enjoy life in a region of wonderful scenic beauty and pleasing climate and will live comfortably in a rural community equipped with the conveniences of town" (1910 ORN booklet). This is the area of the Spitzenburg apple, among others. The city of Hood River is the greatest apple-shipping point in the country. (Above) 1912: Looking north on Second Street. Cross street (ahead) is Oak. Some of the buildings shown: Carl F. Sumner, W. J. Baker Company run by William Baker, drug store with Charles N. Clarke as proprietor. (Below) 1912: Looking west on Oak Street. Cross street is Second. Automobile to left is 1912 EMF. Some of the buildings shown are Butler Banking Company, Leslie Butler, president; Apple Land & Orchard Company, P. S. Davidson, secretary; Arthur Clarke, Jeweler; Fashion Livery & Dray Company under Bert Stranahan and C. B. Rathbun; Lost Lake Lumber Company, W. F. Davidson, president; Roland D. Gould and Frank B. Snyder, Plumbing.

Alfred Mott for many years worked with The Dalles Department of Sanitation. Each day he reversed his working shoes, as this allowed them to last much longer. Note: Shoes are reversed.

The Dalles 1890: *Times Mountaineer* The oldest paper east of the Cascade Mountains. The Dalles *Mountaineer* started in 1862. The Dalles *Times* started in 1880. The two papers merged in 1882 and continued publication until 1904. (Left to right): Otto Peiper, Robert Fleck, J. Frank Haworth, Rose Mitchell, Catherine A. Craig, owner and editor, John Mitchell, Col. C. E. Morgan, unknown.

The Dalles 1879-1929 The Umatilla House: This hotel is considered by many to be one of the finest north of San Francisco, with a fascinating but lurid past. *West Shore* reports, "The building is 100 by 120 feet and cost nearly $35,000. The office is 30 x 40 feet and contains the handsomest counter and most elegant key rack in the state. It has 123 sleeping apartments, with a bathroom on both the second and third floors. The hotel is far above average of what one would expect to find at a place like The Dalles having but 2,600 inhabitants." The Dalles was a stopping point for the steamboats from Portland and made a connection with the stages leaving for central Oregon, for eastern Oregon, and for those going to the mines in Idaho. Later, with the coming of the railroad, it was used to feed rail travelers, as the train stopped directly in front of the building. The hotel was torn down in 1929. (Above) Outside of the hotel, showing Union Pacific tracks passing near the front door. (Below) Main office and waiting room. Dining room can be seen in back. Note interesting stove with its heating apparatus.

233

Fossil's main street (Wheeler County): It is believed W. W. Hoover and Charles F. Iremonger are sitting in the front seat of the 1911 Overland. The rear automobile is a 1911 or 1912 EMF. Man with white shirt is believed to be E. M. Clymer, the postmaster.

The water wagon was often seen during the harvest season around Ione (Morrow County), a small farming community in eastern Oregon. Tanks of water were consumed by the cookhouses, the animals, and the threshing crews. The harvest often lasted sixty days. Combines were pulled by as many as thirty-six horses or mules, and farm wells often went dry. Note saloon in background — always a safeguard in case of a water shortage.

Government Camp (above), located at the foot of Mount Hood, has nothing to do with the government. It's a 320-acre enclave entirely surrounded by the Mount Hood National Forest. Lots that sold here for $75 in the late 1940s are now priced at nearly $10,000. A 1928 Sandwich & Pie Shop, one of many such places at *Government Camp.* Automobiles shown are (left to right) 1926 Willys Knight, 1924 Star, 1926 Chrysler, 1924 Model T Ford, 1923 Jordan.